Taxing and
Spending Policy

Taxing and Spending Policy

Edited by
Warren J. Samuels
Michigan State University

Larry L. Wade
University of California

LexingtonBooks
D.C. Heath and Company
Lexington, Massachusetts
Toronto

Library of Congress Cataloging in Publication Data

Main entry under title:

Taxing and spending policy.

    1.   Finance, Public—United States—Addresses, essays, lectures. 2. Fiscal policy—United States—Addresses, essays, lectures. 3. Taxation—United States—Addresses, essays, lectures. I. Samuels, Warren J., 1933- II. Wade, Larry L.
HJ257.2.T39   336.73   79-3689
ISBN 0-669-03469-x

Copyright © 1980 by D.C. Heath and Company

Published simultaneously in Canada

Printed in the United States of America

International Standard Book Number: 0-669-03469-x

Library of Congress Catalog Card Number: 79-3689

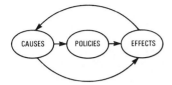

Policy Studies Organization Series

General Approaches to Policy Studies

Specific Policy Problems

Analyzing Poverty Policy
    edited by Dorothy Buckton James
Crime and Criminal Justice
    edited by John A. Gardiner and Michael Mulkey
Civil Liberties
    edited by Stephen L. Wasby
Foreign Policy Analysis
    edited by Richard L. Merritt
Economic Regulatory Policies
    edited by James E. Anderson
Political Science and School Politics
    edited by Samuel K. Gove and Frederick M. Wirt
Science and Technology Policy
    edited by Joseph Haberer
Population Policy Analysis
    edited by Michael E. Kraft and Mark Schneider
The New Politics of Food
    edited by Don F. Hadwiger and William P. Browne
New Dimensions to Energy Policy
    edited by Robert Lawrence
Race, Sex, and Policy Problems
    edited by Marian Lief Palley and Michael Preston
American Security Policy and Policy-Making
    edited by Robert Harkavy and Edward Kolodziej
Current Issues in Transportation Policy
    edited by Alan Altshuler
Security Policies of Developing Countries
    edited by Edward Kolodziej and Robert Harkavy
Determinants of Law-Enforcement Policies
    edited by Fred A. Meyer, Jr., and Ralph Baker
Evaluating Alternative Law-Enforcement Policies
    edited by Ralph Baker and Fred A. Meyer, Jr.
International Energy Policy
    edited by Robert M. Lawrence and Martin O. Heisler
Employment and Labor-Relations Policy
    edited by Charles Bulmer and John L. Carmichael, Jr.
Housing Policy for the 1980s
    edited by Roger Montgomery and Dale Rogers Marshall
Environmental Policy Formation
    edited by Dean E. Mann
Environmental Policy Implementation
    edited by Dean E. Mann

To Joyce and Sylvia

Contents

Acknowledgments

We very much want to express our gratitude for the cooperation and guidance provided by Stuart S. Nagel in the process of preparing this book. We also want to thank the contributors for their efforts and their cooperative and responsive attitude.

Introduction

Taxing and spending is a vast and complex subject that encompasses all of public finance, a field to which the whole of economic theory is being applied, and much of that great part of political science concerned with the processes and content of governmental decision making. Because of its scope, intrinsic difficulty, and substantive importance, the subject is closed at very few if any points. Controversies abound concerning the content of empirical reality (that is, what policy actually is in numerous areas), the implications of existing and conceivable policy for various objectives (for example, equity, efficiency, employment, and balance of payments), and how policy is shaped and developed in the political arena.

Fortunately, there is agreement on one vital point: the subject is not the monopoly of any particular academic discipline or perspective but the appropriate domain of economics, political science, and the other social disciplines, and certainly history and philosophy as well. The contributors to this book are drawn from economics and political-science backgrounds, suggesting immediately no effort at comprehensiveness, but they do illustrate the ferment and intellectual vitality of the field. No universally acceptable model, no common approach to the subject, infuses all the chapters, though the predominant neoclassical framework is common among the economists' contributions. Various research techniques and conceptual frameworks animate the studies by political scientists, who work for the most part with middle-range propositions that sometimes confound popular wisdom. The first objective of this book is to stimulate scholars to examine the work of others who deal with related questions and problems from different methodological perspectives, who ask different questions of the same data, or who generate new data of relevance to those working within different paradigms.

The second goal is to present the reader with new and important findings bearing on substantively important policy issues. The studies by no means exhaust the problems that might have been addressed, but they do touch upon many key problems in contemporary public finance.

Chapter 1 alerts the reader to approach the subject of government growth with care. Despite views advanced on both sides of the question by respected authorities, Attiat F. Ott concludes that measurement problems make it difficult to know whether the growth of government in Western liberal societies has been halted or is still in a process of expansion, a question of great importance to current ideological and policy debates.

Chapter 2 performs a most useful service in a trend analysis of federal expenditures, suggesting that the social, economic, and political forces that have produced recent federal budgets are not of immediate origin but have been at work since at least the end of World War II (and, one suspects, perhaps longer). Chapter 3 demonstrates, contrary to some overexpansion hypotheses, that federal income taxes have been tacitly indexed since 1950, while the ratio of state income taxes to gross national product (GNP) has risen 740 percent, though they do not include all federal tax receipts (such as social security). Progressive tax rates and inflation have significantly influenced the growth of state and local government expenditures in the postwar period. In chapter 4, a rather different focus on revenue elasticity in the states points to additional factors influencing expansions in state and local government. During 1960–1970, spending increased most in states with the least elastic revenue sources, suggesting, among other things, that some states were politically able to impose tax increases without relying on highly elastic revenue systems.

Chapter 5 tests the political argument that civil turmoil, specifically the urban riots of the 1960s, induces increased welfare spending in an effort to buy peace. Edward T. Jennings, Jr., finds that, if such a relationship exists, it is an uneasy one: state welfare spending did not increase following the urban explosion, though spending from federal grants may have been so influenced. Jennings illustrates the difficulty in presuming any simple connection between social events, or public demands, and institutional/political responses.

Along a different line, chapter 6 examines Latin American executives, both civilian and military, and their administration of aggregate public expenditures. Barry Ames finds a kind of political expenditure cycle as executives respond to sociopolitical conditions as well as to their own ideologies in order to maximize support. Not unexpectedly, public expenditures are the means to survival in office.

In addressing the normative bases of tax reform, Michael L. Goetz suggests that from a constitutional perspective tax policy is properly a continuous process, to be adjusted in the light of changing circumstances. There is no "one best" fisc that can be selected at the time of constitutional construction. This healthy pragmatism is reflected in the question dealt with in chapter 8, one which has received considerable attention in recent public debates: "Can a tax cut pay for itself?" At least with respect to capital-gains-tax cuts, Gerald E. Auten concludes that a positive answer cannot now be supported. This chapter illustrates the type of analysis that should be undertaken before presuming the revenue consequences of reductions in other types of taxes.

The complex issue of government deficits and their financing is addressed in chapter 9. The constraints on government may not be assumed often in analyses that point to domestic capital markets and monetization of the deficit as the only sources of debt management. These alternatives have important implications for both monetary and fiscal policy. Chapter 10 describes the interactions between monetary and fiscal policy (a distinction arising as much from institutional as from theoretical reasons) and argues that contemporary policy has tilted toward consumption, leading to higher interest rates and less capital formation than would arise from a policy of balanced budgets or debt retirement. These grand issues, obviously, are dealt with by politicians and political institutions, and several political scientists have contributed studies that shed light on certain of their dimensions.

Ideology played an important role in shaping the outcome of the Revenue Act of 1978. Chapter 11 also reminds us that tax policy is a traditional congressional monopoly, resistant to presidential initiatives for reform. Economic analysis must take such realities into account. At the same time, chapter 12 examines the impact of the 1974 Congressional Budget Reform Act and concludes that its intent, to increase congressional influence over appropriations, has not yet been realized. With regard to taxing and spending policy, recent efforts at change have shown the tenaciousness of traditional practices.

With respect to state tax preferences, chapter 13 concludes that states with competitive partisan alignments have placed personal-income taxes lower in their preference orderings than other types of taxes. This is a non-obvious and rather confounding finding, since political scientists would normally predict that competitive policies (suggesting the mobilization of the less advantaged) would lead to more progressive modes of taxation.

Also on the subject of tax preferences, chapter 14 suggests that political and life-style factors have a greater influence on individuals' tax preferences than do economic self-interest factors. Moreover, economic self-interest seems to influence income- and sales-tax preferences in a manner opposite to the anticipated pattern. Ideology, party affiliation, urban-rural life-style, and education (in order of influence) play a dominant role in explaining individuals' income- and sales-tax preferences.

The analysis in chapter 15 of three alternative hypotheses governing tax decisions at the individual level focuses upon the failure of the Tisch amendment in Michigan (a Proposition 13 clone). David Lowery's data fail to confirm two conventional economic explanations of voter-taxpayer choice, and point to the importance of political culture (or social-psychological attributes) in framing individual choice. Although it is by no means definitive, his study illustrates the importance of informing economic models with empirical information on voter ideology.

Chapter 16 presents an analysis of the regional benefits from federal spending that is fraught with political implications. The multiplier effects of different types of federal spending are examined in addition to per capita spending. Should their implications be considered by political decision makers, old disputes may take on additional dimensions.

Chapter 17 undertakes the difficult and much-needed task of integrating the diverse strands of externality, public goods, and grants theories. The ubiquity of interdependence is stressed, and a normatively neutral scheme is advanced by which policymakers might be assisted in estimating the individual and social impacts of various actions. The concluding chapter examines the understanding of fiscal politics advanced from what Larry L. Wade contends is an excessively simplified, nonempirical, and often mistaken rational-choice perspective. He argues that economic approaches to fiscal decision making must include data that are more subtle, complex, and consistent with the empirical findings of political science.

In combination, the several chapters illustrate the range of problems that invite further work. The field, obviously, is open and receptive to contributions from many quarters. It is our hope that readers will be stimulated and encouraged to assume some part of the many tasks that remain for better understanding of taxing and spending policy.

**Part I
The Growth of
Public Spending**

1

Has the Growth of Government in the West Been Halted?

Attiat F. Ott

In one of his popular and provocative articles Milton Friedman asks: can we halt leviathan?[1] Citing statistics on government spending in the United States, Friedman reported total government spending to have risen from less than 15 percent of national income in 1930 to about 40 percent in 1972. Based on this empirical observation, he states that "neither legislated ceilings nor any other administrative device will halt leviathan." The claim that government in the West has been growing rapidly is shared by many others. In a recent American Enterprise Institute publication, G. Warren Nutter made the claim that the "growth of government seems universal in the West."[2]

Using a sample of sixteen Western democracies, Nutter investigated what has happened over the last quarter-century to expenditures at all levels of government as a percentage of national income. His calculations showed the median percentage of national income absorbed by governments in these countries to have risen from 34 percent in 1953 to 49 percent in 1973. This finding led him to conclude that "if government continues to grow in the United States at merely the established trend, within another decade or two it will rival its size at the peak for World War II, without the need of a war to make it so large."[3]

Has government been growing rapidly? Although the above cited statistics support this contention, they have been challenged.[4] Here, we seek to investigate, in somewhat more detail, the growth of government in the United States and in five other major Western democracies. This study focuses particularly on the conflicting evidence on public-sector growth. It concludes with a discussion of some of the problems involved in measuring and comparing the size of government over time.

Measuring the Growth of Government

The first question one has to grapple with is how to measure the size of government. Should it be measured by the level of fiscal actions, or in terms of resources absorbed by the government directly through the budget and indirectly through private-sector compliance? Because many of these indirect costs are not readily available, a narrower measure of the scope of government activity has been commonly used.[5] In this chapter the ratio of the public sector's spending to the nation's output has been used to measure the resource-absorbing activity of governments. In tables 1-1 through 1-4, government activities and their relation to gross domestic product (GDP) for the six Organization for Economic Cooperation and Development (OECD) countries are presented. The six OECD countries are the United States, Canada, France, Germany, the United Kingdom, and Sweden.

When their growth is measured in current prices (table 1-1), it is evident that governments in the West have been growing very rapidly. The mean ratio of total government spending to GDP has risen from an average of 28.9 percent in 1950-1952 to 48.8 percent in 1973-1975. This evidence is not supported, however, when the growth of government is measured in real terms. Comparing the average mean ratio of government spending to GDP in the 1950-1952 period with those of the 1970-1973 or 1973-1975 periods, it appears as if the growth of government has been halted. The ratio of government spending to GDP fell from 37.9 percent in the mid-1950s to 35.4 percent in the early 1970s. The 1973-1975 ratio of 36.3 percent is almost the same as that calculated for the 1950-1952 period.

These contradictory findings give rise to a fundamental if not crucial measurement question; that is, should we measure the size of government by the real resources it claims or by the value of the resources used? Although both measurements are reported here (nominal and real values), we believe that the size of government is best measured by the amount of resources it claims and not by how much it pays for them.

It is worth noting at this point that, although the mean ratio of real spending to GDP has remained fairly constant, the ratio of public spending to GDP in each of the six OECD countries has not. Furthermore budget priorities have not remained constant throughout the period. As table 1-2 shows, the mean ratio of real-transfer payments to total spending has risen from 21.4 percent in 1950 to 33.5 percent in 1975, whereas government investment and consumption outlays have fallen or remained fairly constant in the countries studied.

Additional evidence on the growth of governments is given in tables 1-3 and 1-4. Except for transfer payments (where the growth rates have by far outdistanced those of GDP), the growth rates of real spending have barely exceeded the growth rates of real GDP. Variations between countries in their respective growth rates over the whole period and for each subperiod are noticeable, however. In Germany, the long-run average annual rates of growth of public spending were consistently below those of GDP during both the decades of the 1950s and the 1960s. In France, the real-growth rates of total spending were consistently below those of GDP, while in the United States they lagged behind GDP only in the 1960-1970 era.

Table 1-1
Government Spending as a Percentage of Gross Domestic Product in Current and Constant Prices and for Selected Periods

Country	Current Prices				Constant Prices[a]			
	Average of 1950–1952	Average of 1955–1958	Average of 1970–1973	Average of 1973–1975	Average of 1950–1952	Average of 1955–1958	Average of 1970–1973	Average of 1973–1975
Canada	23.7	27.1	36.6	38.7	34.6	35.5	35.2	36.7
France	30.0	33.4	37.8	39.9	41.3	42.3	36.7	36.7
Germany	30.5	31.0	37.3	41.9	42.6	39.3	35.7	37.0
United Kingdom	35.0	32.1	46.9	43.9	45.3	39.8	37.8	39.3
United States	25.2	26.9	32.7	34.1	32.6	32.8	31.5	31.6
Mean ratio	(28.9)	(30.1)	(38.3)	(39.7)	(36.5)	(37.9)	(35.4)	(36.3)
Sweden	NA	NA	44.9	48.8	NA	NA	43.3	44.3

Source: OECD, *National Accounts of OECD Countries*, 1950–1968 and 1962–1975.
Note: Total government expenditures in constant prices were obtained by deflating components of public spending by the appropriate price index, that is, transfer payments were deflated by using the consumer price index whereas the government-purchases deflator was used to deflate government purchases.
[a]1970 prices.

Table 1-2
Budget Allocation in the United States and Five Other OECD Countries, 1950–1975
(constant 1970 prices; percent)

Country	Transfer Payments			Consumption Outlays			Outlays for Capital Formation		
	Average of 1950–1960	Average of 1961–1970	Average of 1971–1975	Average of 1950–1960	Average of 1961–1970	Average of 1971–1975	Average of 1950–1960	Average of 1961–1970	Average of 1971–1975
United States	13.9	20.5	31.7	66.1	68.1	62.1	10.8	9.9	6.8
Canada	17.4	20.4	27.6	51.2	61.5	60.7	12.1	13.1	10.0
France	31.6	44.2	47.8	43.3	38.3	37.6	6.9	9.0	4.5
Germany	30.4	29.8	35.8	44.0	46.1	49.7	8.4	11.6	9.6
United Kingdom	13.6	20.3	24.7	51.7	52.7	56.2	11.5	12.0	11.8
Sweden	NA	24.2	33.3	NA	61.3	54.0	NA	14.8	10.6
Mean[a]	21.4	27.0	33.5	51.3	53.3	53.3	9.9	11.1	8.5

Source: OECD, *National Accounts of OECD Countries*, 1950–1968 and 1962–1975.
[a] Excluding Sweden.

Table 1-3
Compounding Growth Rates of Output and Government Spending
(1950-1975)

Country	Current Prices					Constant Prices				
	GDP	G	G_c	TR	G_I	GDP	G	G_c	TR	G_I
Canada	7.8	15.7	19.5	16.5	5.0	2.2	2.9	3.7	6.2	2.1
France	13.0	20.4	16.5	22.4	24.0	2.3	2.1	1.5	4.8	4.0
Germany	9.7	14.1	15.7	11.8	19.5	3.0	2.7	2.8	5.0	4.1
United Kingdom	7.0	10.3	11.7	14.0	15.0	0.9	0.8	1.0	2.7	1.4
United States	4.2	7.7	8.5	9.1	4.4	1.3	1.6	1.8	3.5	0.6

Source: OECD, *National Accounts of OECD Countries*, 1950–1968 and 1962–1975.
Note: The growth rate is calculated as follows: $(G_t /G_o - 1)$, where G_t is the end of the period and G_o is the beginning of the period. Growth rates were not calculated for Sweden for lack of data for the earlier period.
    GDP = gross domestic product; G = total government spending; G_c = government consumption; TR = transfer payments; and G_I = government spending for capital formation.

Income Elasticity of Public Spending

Because the data reported in the previous tables exhibit some variability in the behavior of the public sector among the countries examined, it may be useful to look at some other indicators for intercountry comparisons. The income elasticity of public spending is a useful indicator of the relationship betwen the growth of income and the change in the demand for public services. An income elasticity of demand greater than one would indicate that a given rise in income produces a larger increase in the demand for public expenditure; a value of less than one would indicate the opposite. For the six OECD countries three separate expenditure functions have been estimated. The regression equation specifies that the level of real public spending at time t depends on permanent income and other variables assumed to be captured by a time trend. After looking at the data relationship, we have elected to estimate the regression equations in linear form, and then use the regression coefficients and the mean values of the variables to compute the elasticity coefficients. The estimated elasticities are presented in table 1-5.

    The findings reported in the table warrant the following observations:

1. The relationship between public expenditure and income is *not* invariant with respect to the type of public spending.

Table 1–4

Long-Run Growth Rates of Output and Government Spending in Constant Prices

(average annual rate of growth; percent)

Country	Growth Rates				
	GDP	*G*	*G_c*	*TR*	*G_I*
	1950–1975				
Canada	4.8	4.8	5.4	7.5	4.6
France	5.0	4.5	3.5	7.1	6.4
Germany	5.7	5.2	5.5	6.1	6.8
United Kingdom	2.8	2.2	2.7	5.8	2.6
United States	3.4	3.2	3.1	7.4	1.3
Sweden	4.3	NA	5.0	8.1	NA
	1950–1960				
Canada	3.8	4.6	3.7	9.3	8.2
France	4.6	4.3	2.6	7.5	8.3
Germany	7.6	6.6	4.7	10.0	11.3
United Kingdom	2.6	0.3	0.8	5.3	−0.6
United States	2.8	3.0	3.2	4.9	4.0
Sweden	3.5	NA	4.5	7.0	NA
	1960–1970				
Canada	5.6	5.1	6.7	6.5	2.9
France	4.9	4.9	3.8	7.8	5.6
Germany	4.6	3.9	4.3	3.7	3.8
United Kingdom	2.9	8.2	3.1	6.4	6.1
United States	4.4	3.8	3.6	7.9	1.4
Sweden	4.7	5.8	5.6	8.9	6.9
	1970–1975				
Canada	4.7	6.0	4.3	10.2	4.6
France	3.9	3.7	3.0	5.1	−0.6
Germany	2.1	3.6	4.7	8.3	−2.7
United Kingdom	2.3	3.6	3.0	5.1	0.7
United States	2.4	2.6	1.4	8.2	−2.0
Sweden	2.6	3.8	3.1	10.3	−6.8

Source: OECD, *National Accounts of OECD Countries,* 1950–1968 and 1962–1975.

Note: Long-run annual growth rates were estimated from the following regression equation: $\text{Log } X_i = \alpha_o + \alpha_1 T$, where X_i = variable i (such as GDP); α_o = constant; α_1 = growth rate; T = time.

2. With the exception of the United Kingdom, the income elasticity of demand for public goods of the consumption type falls short of one, ranging from 0.525 in the United States to 0.852 in Canada.
3. The United Kingdom experience during the period seems to be unlike most of the other OECD countries. The income elasticity coefficient was found to be greater than one for three parameters.

Table 1–5
Estimates of the Income Elasticity of Public Spending (1950–1975)

Country	Variable		
	G	G_c	TR
Canada	0.455	0.852	− 0.047
	(1.08)[a]	(3.70)	(− 0.04)
France	0.380	0.630	0.560
	(2.70)	(5.21)	(3.03)
Germany	− 0.04	0.830	− 1.59
	(− 0.15)	(2.30)	(2.27)
United Kingdom	1.80	1.70	2.82
	(2.70)	(1.5)	(6.30)
United States	0.540	0.525	− 1.15
	(2.20)	(2.70)	(− 1.80)
Sweden			1.90[b]
			(− 3.3)

Source: OECD, *National Accounts of OECD Countries*, 1950–1968 and 1962–1975.
[a] Student = t values in parentheses.
[b] Due to lack of data other elasticities were not computed.

Conflicting Evidence on the Growth of Public Spending

Conflicting evidence regarding the growth of government in the West abounds in the recent literature. Until Beck's findings (1976),[6] most studies seem to suggest a continued trend of public-sector activities. Beck, however, offered evidence which did suggest that the era of public-sector growth in the developed economies has come to an end or stabilized. For thirteen OECD countries he has shown a decline in the real size of the public sector between 1950 and 1970. He also found that the income elasticity of real-government expenditures to be less than unity in eight of the thirteen OECD countries.

Beck's findings were challenged by Dubin.[7] Using the same (unde-flated) data series as those used by Beck but applying the government-purchases deflator to deflate government consumption and the private-consumption deflator to deflate transfer payments, Dubin recalculated Beck's ratios. His calculations reversed Beck's findings. In eleven out of twelve OECD nations, the ratio of real government expenditure to real GDP was shown to have increased between 1950 and 1970, though it was not found to be as spectacular as when the rate is calculated in nominal terms.

In a later study Beck (1979) recomputed the ratio of government spending to GDP utilizing a different procedure to deflate government spending.[8] Unlike his earlier article he deflated each component of public spending by a separate price deflator before arriving at the real value of public spending. His experimentation with published deflators as well as others led him to decompose (for the purpose of deflating) spending into compensation of employees, purchases from private firms, and transfer outlays. Capital outlays were excluded from the total in calculating real outlays.

From the ratios calculated, Beck computed an income elasticity of public spending between 1950 and 1974. His findings again reinforced his earlier contention that the size of the public sector seems to have been stabilized. Between 1950 and 1974 the median share of real-consumption expenditures rose slightly from 12.1 percent in 1950 to 12.4 percent in 1974. The median value of the elasticity coefficient was found to be around 0.79.

Wagner and Weber estimated, using a sample of thirty-four developed and developing countries, the compounding growth rates of public expenditures and GDP, as well as the income elasticity of demand for public spending during the period 1950-1972.[9] The evidence obtained in their study is not conclusive, however. In some countries the cumulative growth rates of total public spending for consumption-type outlays have exceeded those of GDP, while they were less than GDP in other countries. Furthermore, the income elasticity coefficient found by Wagner and Weber was not consistently above or below unity.

Nutter,[10] using a sample of sixteen Western countries, showed the median percentage of national income (rather than GDP) absorbed by governments to have risen from 34 percent in 1953 to 49 percent in 1973.

To focus more clearly on this contradictory evidence, we present in tables 1-6 and 1-7 a summary comparison of the findings available in the literature. To make the findings comparable with one another, Nutter's spending ratios were recomputed as percentages of GDP rather than national income. In table 1-6 the current and deflated spending ratios are given. In table 1-7 the ratios of deflated current (spending on current account) government spending to real GDP as reported by Beck (1976) and by Dubin are compared with one another and with ratios calculated for this study.

From table 1-6 it is clear that governments in the West have been growing over the past quarter-century if that growth is measured in nominal terms. When expressed in real terms the ratio of real spending to GDP is found to have risen in only three countries in the sample: Canada, Denmark, and the Netherlands. The findings reported in table 1-7 are not conclusive; they neither support nor refute the growth hypothesis. For example, Beck's findings indicate that the ratio of current government spending to output had fallen between 1950-1952 and 1969-1970. The mean ratio of

Table 1-6
Total Government Spending as a Percentage of Gross Domestic Product in Ten OECD Countries

Country	In Current Prices			In Constant (1970) Prices		
	Average of 1950–1952	Average of 1970–1973	Direction of Change	Average of 1950–1952	Average of 1970–1973	Direction of Change
Austria	27.4	36.2	+	50.4	34.9	−
Canada	23.7	36.6	+	34.6	35.2	+
Denmark	21.4	41.0	+	33.1	39.1	+
Finland	24.4	33.1	+	34.1	32.3	−
France	30.0	37.8	+	41.3	36.7	−
Germany	30.5	37.3	+	42.6	35.7	−
Netherlands	27.0	46.5	+	43.9	44.5	+
Sweden	NA	44.9		NA	43.3	
United Kingdom	35.0	46.9	+	45.3	37.8	−
United States	25.2	32.7	+	32.6	31.5	−
Mean[a]	(27.3)	(38.7)	+	(39.8)	(36.4)	−

Source: OECD, *National Accounts of OECD Countries,* 1950–1968 and 1962–1975.
Note: Due to lack of data on total spending for the entire period only nine countries from the Nutter Sample of sixteen countries are represented in the table.
[a] Excluding Sweden.

public spending fell from 24.1 to 23.5 percent. When a different set of price deflators was used, this finding was not supported, however. Dubin's data show the ratio of current government spending to GDP rose from a mean value of 23.7 percent in 1950–1952 to 28 percent in 1968–1970. Our ratios (calculated using separate deflators of public spending and based on 1970 prices) seem to support Beck's and refute Dubin's.

The sensitivity of the findings to the choice of the price deflator complicates the testing of the growth hypothesis. This complexity raises two questions: should the size and thus the growth of government be measured in real terms, and which deflator should be used for deflating government spending? Since we lack uniformly constructed deflators for deflating total or components of government spending in several countries, one may argue that the controversy is far from being settled. What is certain from these findings, however, is that when the growth of government is measured in nominal terms, it remains true that governments in the West have been growing very rapidly.

Table 1-7
Comparisons of Ratios of Current Government Expenditures to GDP in Constant Prices (base period 1950–1952 and 1970)

Country	Beck Study[a] (1950–1952 Prices)		Dubin[b] (1950–1952 Prices)			Ott (1970 Prices)		
	1950–1952	1968–1970	1950–1952	1968–1970	1970–1973	1950–1952	1968–1970	1970–1973
Austria	23.5	16.2	23.6	26.1	25.1	42.7	31.7	29.0
Canada	21.3	19.8	21.3	25.6	28.2	34.6	35.0	35.2
Denmark	19.6	22.0	19.6	27.2	30.0	30.4	33.4	33.9
Finland	19.3	20.3	19.3	23.4	24.0	26.0	28.5	27.8
France	32.5	24.4	28.3	30.1	34.4	41.3	40.3	36.7
Germany	28.5	23.1	28.5	29.3	30.4	42.6	37.3	35.7
Greece	19.1	12.7	19.1	19.2	19.0	20.4	20.9	19.9
Netherlands	24.1	22.3	24.1	36.0	37.7	38.8	38.0	39.1
Switzerland	19.6	18.4	NA	NA	NA	18.1	18.9	19.8
Sweden	23.2	32.7	23.2	30.8	33.9	25.5	34.0	36.3
United Kingdom	30.7	25.3	30.7	33.6	33.9	45.3	39.3	37.8
United States	22.8	23.8	22.8	26.8	26.7	32.6	32.6	31.5
Mean ratio[c]	(24.1)	(23.5)	(23.7)	(28.0)	(29.4)	(34.6)	(33.7)	(33.0)

Note: Current expenditures refer to current disbursement of general government which includes government consumption, transfer payments, subsidies, interest on public debt, and miscellaneous current expenditures.

[a] Morris Beck, "The Expanding Public Sector: Some Contrary Evidence," *National Tax Journal* (March 1976):17.
[b] Elliot Dubin, "The Expanding Public Sector: Some Contrary Evidence—A Comment," *National Tax Journal* (March 1977):75.
[c] Excluding Switzerland.

Notes

1. Milton Friedman, "Can We Halt Leviathan?" *Newsweek,* 6 November 1972.

2. G. Warren Nutter, *Growth of Government in the West* (Washington, D.C.: American Enterprise Institute, 1978).

3. Ibid., p. 18.

4. Morris Beck, "The Expanding Public Sector: Some Contrary Evidence," *National Tax Journal* (March 1976): 15–21.

5. James C. Miller, III, and Murray L. Widenbaum attempted to measure some of these costs. See, for example, James C. Miller, III, "Regulatory Reform: Some Problems and Approaches" (Washington, D.C.: American Enterprise Institute, Reprint No. 72, August 1977).

6. Beck, "Expanding Public Sector."

7. Elliott Dubin, "The Expanding Public Sector: Some Contrary Evidence—A Comment," National Tax Journal (March 1977): 95.

8. Morris Beck, "Inflation, Government Spending, and Real Size of the Public Sector," *Atlantic Economic Journal* 3 (September 1979): 25–34.

9. Richard E. Wagner and Warren E. Weber, "Wagner's Law, Fiscal Institutions, and the Growth of Government," *National Tax Journal* (1977): 59–68.

10. Nutter, *Growth of Government.*

Appendix 1 A:
Data Methods

All the data used in this study and in Dubin's were obtained from OECD, *National Accounts of OECD Countries.* Beck utilized two data sources: United Nations, *Yearbook of National Accounts Statistics,* and OECD, *National Accounts of OECD Countries.* The deflated-data series differ in the three studies because of the selection of the base year or the choice of the price deflator to deflate government spending. To get real current public spending, Beck used the implicit price deflator for government final consumption to deflate all components of current spending. Dubin chose to deflate the components of government spending by separate deflators. He argues that because governments have the option of either buying goods and services and then redistributing them to specific groups of the population or supplying them with an equivalent amount in cash, we should therefore distinguish between these two types of activities. Accordingly, Dubin utilized the implicit price deflator for final government consumption to deflate final government consumption while utilizing the implicit price deflator for private consumption expenditures to deflate all other current expenditures (the largest being transfer payments).

2

Trends and Cycles in the Composition of the Federal Budget, 1947–1978

Ronald L. Teigen

Introduction

A good deal of attention has been given to the growth of the federal budget, in absolute terms and relative to gross national product (GNP), since World War II. Somewhat less notice has been paid to the shifts that have occurred in the budget's composition during this time, but these compositional changes have been considerable and have important social-welfare implications. The purpose here is to measure, in summary fashion, the extent to which trend, cyclical, and other systematic forces have brought about changes in budget shares during the postwar era.

Let us begin with a brief review of the actual changes in budget composition during these years. Table 2–1 shows the fraction of each National Income Account (NIA) expenditure and revenue category to the total in 1947 and again in 1978, and indicates the category's growth rate over the period. Among the expenditures, the budget shares of domestic transfers to persons and grants-in-aid to state and local governments have risen sharply, while defense purchases, foreign transfers, and net interest have fallen. In the tax categories, corporate and indirect taxes have lost position, while the share of social-insurance contributions has risen from about one-eighth to one-third of total receipts. In some categories there occurred quite a lot of movement during the period opposite in direction to the long-run changes captured by these endpoint data. For instance, the share comprised of military purchases rose from 30.3 percent of total expenditures in 1947 to 58 percent in 1951 before beginning a steady decline. This rapid increase was of course due to the Korean War; by contrast, during the Vietnam period defense purchases did not rise nearly as sharply in relative terms. The budget share represented by domestic transfers to persons fell very sharply from 29.5 percent in 1947 to 14.8 percent in 1951 (due mostly to a decline in the size of veterans' programs) before beginning to rise steadily to its present share of 39.4 percent. And the income and corporate-profits tax shares show evidence of cyclical movement.

The author gratefully acknowledges support provided by the Research Seminar in Quantitative Economics, University of Michigan, and the able assistance of David Garman.

Procedure

To investigate the systematic forces which affect the budget's makeup without actually modeling in detail the determinants of each spending and tax program, we will use a procedure which has been applied to the analysis of income distribution patterns.[1] Under this approach, budget shares are regressed directly on a time trend (summarizing a set of social, political, demographic, economic, and other factors exerting systematic, long-run effects on shares), a variable representing cyclical movements in the economy (the unemployment rate is used here), and other regressors standing for forces or events which have affected significantly the budget's composition. The rate of inflation is included because expenditures under a number of programs (for example, social security, civil service, and military retirement) are mechanically indexed for inflation, while other programs appear to be adjusted systematically for price change though not via a formal indexing procedure; and tax revenues related to nominal income can be viewed as indexed in that revenues will change as the inflation rate changes, other things equal.[2] Finally, the regressions contain dummy variables which reflect abrupt shifts in budget structure. A multiplicative dummy has been inserted as of 1951 to capture the acceleration of outlays which began with the Korean War. An additive expenditure dummy for 1972 represents the startup at that time of general-purpose revenue sharing, a program which went from zero to $6.6 billion of outlays in one year. The tax receipts relationships presumably shift whenever major changes in the tax laws are enacted. A priori, one can identify four such revisions during 1947–1978: the tax reductions of 1948, 1964, and 1975, and the 1968 tax surcharge. While tests for such shifts were conducted in trial regressions, only the dummy for the 1964 tax cut, entered multiplicatively with the time trend, was significant. Its multiplicative form is consistent with the fact that the 1964 tax reduction was accomplished mainly by changing tax rates rather than exemptions or other features of the tax law.

In summary, our regression procedure as applied to expenditure shares is as follows:

$$\left(\frac{E_i}{E} \right)_t = \alpha_i + \beta_{i1}\,\text{Time}_t + \beta_{i2}\,\text{Time}_t \cdot \text{DUM51}_t + \beta_{i3}\,U_t + \beta_{i4}\,\mathring{\Delta}\text{CPI}_{t-\frac{1}{2}}$$

$$+ \beta_{i5}\,\text{DUM72}_t + \epsilon_{it} \qquad (i = 1, 2, \ldots, n)$$

where there are n expenditure categories and where E_i/E is the fraction of the ith expenditure program to total expenditures; Time is a linear time trend; U is the unemployment rate (measuring the effects on the budget of cyclical movements in the economy);[3] $\mathring{\Delta}$CPI is the rate of inflation as mea-

Table 2–1
Compound Annual Growth Rates and Changes in Budget Share for Federal Budget Programs, NIA Budget, 1947–1978

Category	Percent of Total		Compound Annual Growth Rate (percent)
	1947	1978	1947–1978
Expenditures			
Defense purchases of goods and services	30.3	21.6	8.04
Nondefense purchases of goods and services	12.3	11.8	9.09
Domestic transfer payments to persons	29.5	39.4	10.26
Foreign transfer payments	6.5	0.8	1.90
Grants-in-aid to state and local governments	5.9	16.6	12.96
Net interest paid	13.7	7.7	7.23
All other expenditures[a]	1.8	2.1	9.64
Total expenditures			9.23
Revenues			
Personal taxes and nontax receipts	45.4	44.8	7.65
Corporate-profits-tax accruals	24.7	16.6	6.33
Indirect business tax and nontax accruals	18.0	6.5	4.20
Contributions for social insurance	11.9	32.2	11.23
Total revenues			7.70

Source: *The Budget of the United States Government,* various years.
[a] Subsidies less current surpluses of government enterprises, plus wage disbursements less accruals.

sured by the rate of change of the consumer price index (lagged one-half year because mechanically indexed programs typically respond to changes in inflation with a lag of about this length); DUM51 is a dummy variable which is zero from 1947 to 1950 and unity from 1951 to 1978; DUM72 is a dummy variable whose value is zero from 1947 to 1971 and unity from 1972 to 1978; and DUM64 (which appears in the tax equations) is a dummy variable which is zero from 1947 to 1963 and unity from 1964 to 1978.

For tax programs the format is generally the same as above, but the dependent variable becomes T_j / T, the ratio of the jth tax program's receipts to total revenues ($J = 1,2,..., m$ for m revenue programs). Also, as noted above, the dummy variables are different.

It is important to stress that the same specification is used for all the equations for expenditure shares, and similarly for receipts. This is because of the adding-up constraints imposed by the use of the ordinary least squares (OLS) regression procedure. For a set of OLS regressions, all of which use the same explanatory variables and for which the dependent variables are ratios summing to unity, the coefficients estimated for a given explanatory variable will sum to zero across equations. Likewise, the intercepts will sum to unity and the errors as of any point in time sum to zero. Thus, for example, if a one-point increase in the inflation rate causes the share of a given expenditure category to rise by, say, two percentage points, the regression procedure ensures that the combined share of all the other expenditure categories will fall by this amount in response to the inflation change. It is this desirable consistency feature which leads to the inclusion of the same variables in all regressions.

Results

The regression results for expenditure and revenue programs are given in tables 2-2 and 2-3, respectively. Looking first at the overall quality of these estimates, we see that the fits are very good in most cases, with $\bar{R}^2$ values of .8 or higher in eight of eleven estimates. In other words, our simple structure explains almost all of the movement of budget shares over 1947-1978 for most categories. The personal-income-tax equation (3.1) is the only important exception, with an $\bar{R}^2$ of .29. However, this equation shows no evidence of misspecification and performs well on other criteria. Two equations, (2.7) and (3.3), show evidence of serially correlated residuals, possibly biasing the t-values upward. The former equation showed evidence of a structural shift at 1965 using a standard stability test. In reestimates over the subperiods before and after 1965, the time trend and indexing variables became insignificant in 1965-1978, while the variable Time·DUM51 alone was significant. In any case, this is not an important category. A reestimate of (3.3) with a correction for autocorrelation produced an autoregressive parameter of .6, but no qualitative change in the results and indeed very little change in the numerical estimates. Consequently it is not reported.

Regarding forces systematically influencing budget composition, these estimates indicate that there have been significant upward-trend movements in the shares of nondefense purchases (0.197 percentage points per year since 1951), domestic transfer payments (0.715 points), and grants-in-aid (0.428 points). Taken together, the share of these programs has been rising 1.34 percentage points per year due to trend factors; and this more than accounts for the increase in their combined share from 47.7 to 67.8 percent over 1947-1978.[4] Significant negative trends are displayed by defense purchases, whose share has been falling trendwise 1.29 percentage points per year since 1951; foreign transfer payments (0.123 points); and net interest (0.002 points). The combined share of these programs has shown a negative trend totaling 1.42 points per year—just slightly greater than that of the upward-trending group.

As to other significant systematic effects, the share of defense purchases shows a procyclical response, while domestic transfers move coun-

Table 2-2
Regression Results for Expenditures Share Equations, NIA Budget Data, 1947–1978

Equation Number	Dependent Variable	Intercept	Time	Time + DUM51	Unemployment Rate	$\overset{\circ}{A}CPI$ $-\frac{1}{2}$	DUM72	$\bar{R}^2$	Standard Error	Mean of Dependent Variable	Durbin-Watson Statistic
(2.1)	E_{Def}/E	25.959 (18.047)	−0.0131 (−17.720)	0.00016 (19.952)	−0.0098 (−2.991)	−0.0038 (−2.895)	−0.0210 (−1.431)	.98	.020	0.411	1.41
(2.2)	E_{Nondef}/E	−3.778 (−3.181)	0.0020 (3.300)	−0.00003 (−5.045)	−0.0013 (−0.487)	−0.0002 (−0.160)	−0.0173 (−1.423)	.45	.017	0.113	1.37
(2.3)	E_{DomTr}/E	−13.900 (−10.820)	0.0072 (10.918)	−0.00005 (7.398)	0.0116 (3.965)	0.0033 (2.829)	0.0277 (2.108)	.95	.018	0.259	1.88
(2.4)	E_{ForTr}/E	2.343 (3.303)	−0.0012 (−3.157)	−0.00003 (−7.998)	0.0004 (0.267)	−0.0003 (−0.531)	0.0053 (0.734)	.88	.018	0.028	2.05
(2.5)	E_{Grants}/E	−8.407 (−21.040)	0.0043 (21.110)	−0.00002 (−7.580)	−0.0006 (−0.643)	0.0007 (2.060)	0.0181 (4.441)	.98	.006	0.090	1.14
(2.6)	E_{NetInt}/E	0.347 (0.851)	−0.0001 (−0.572)	−0.00002 (−9.892)	−0.0010 (−1.060)	0.0012 (3.181)	0.0013 (0.314)	.90	.006	0.073	1.51
(2.7)	E_{Other}/E	−1.564 (−3.218)	0.0008 (3.253)	−0.00000 (−0.957)	0.0007 (0.590)	−0.0009 (−2.110)	−0.0141 (−2.848)	.37	.007	0.025	1.01

t-statistics are shown in parentheses below coefficient estimates.
In the above table, E is total budget expenditures (NIA budget), E_{Def} is defense purchases of goods and services, E_{Nondef} is nondefense purchases of goods and services, E_{DomTr} is domestic transfer payments to persons, E_{ForTr} is foreign transfer payments, E_{Grants} is grants-in-aid to state and local governments, E_{NetInt} is net interest paid, and E_{Other} is all other expenditures.

Table 2-3
Regression Results for Tax-Share Equations, NIA Budget Data, 1947–1978

Equation Number	Dependent Variable	Intercept	Time	Time × DUM64	Unemployment Rate	$\overset{\circ}{\Delta}CPI$ $-\frac{1}{2}$	$\bar{R}^2$	Standard Error	Mean of Dependent Variable	Durbin-Watson Statistic
(3.1)	T_{Per}/T	-5.510 (-2.859)	0.0031 (3.090)	-0.00002 (-2.284)	-0.0076 (-2.195)	0.0007 (0.6305)	.29	.020	0.447	1.40
(3.2)	T_{Corp}/T	8.600 (3.877)	-0.0043 (-3.726)	-0.00000 (-0.1400)	-0.0051 (-1.269)	-0.0018 (-1.436)	.80	.023	0.224	1.30
(3.3)	T_{IBT}/T	9.778 (13.661)	-0.0049 (-13.404)	0.00001 (3.196)	0.0052 (4.035)	-0.0013 (-3.247)	.96	.008	0.127	0.95
(3.4)	T_{SocIns}/T	-11.869 (-12.250)	0.0061 (12.289)	0.00001 (2.503)	0.0075 (4.291)	0.0025 (4.432)	.98	.010	0.203	1.63

t-statistics are shown in parentheses below coefficient estimates.

In the above table, T is total budget receipts (NIA budget), T_{Per} is personal taxes and nontax receipts, T_{Corp} is corporate profits tax accruals, T_{IBT} is indirect business tax and nontax accruals, and T_{SocIns} is contributions for social insurance.

tercyclically in approximately the same degree (that is, a one-point unemployment rate change has resulted in a reduction in the defense purchases share of one percentage point, and an increase of one point or so for domestic transfers). We would of course expect domestic transfers to move countercyclically; what is interesting is that ceteris paribus there has been close to a dollar-for-dollar trade-off between defense spending and transfers in response to cyclical forces, according to these estimates. Finally we consider price-indexing effects. Note first that any program which displays, for example, a positive and significant price inflation coefficient is gaining budget share due solely to the effects of inflation. In general, such a program is said to be overindexed. If a program is indexed in such a way as just to maintain its share, ceteris paribus, its inflation-rate coefficient should be insignificantly different from zero. In the particular case of interest payments, a one-point inflation-rate increase should lead to about a one-point rise in market interest rates; that is, to a fairly substantial percentage increase in net interest payments. In our expenditure estimates, we find that defense purchases seem to have been significantly underindexed, while domestic transfers and grants-in-aid together show an almost identical amount of overindexing. Net interest payments have a positive and significant coefficient which indicates that a one-point inflation-rate increase has produced an increase in this category's share of 0.12 percentage points.

All revenue categories show very significant trend movements, with the strongest upward trend in the share of social-insurance contributions (0.61 percentage points per year). The personal-income-tax share is rising trendwise at just half that rate. The shares of corporate and indirect business taxes have been trending downward at almost equal rates, the former declining 0.43 percentage points and the latter 0.49 points per year. Three of the four tax shares show significant cyclical sensitivity, with the personal-tax share varying procyclically as might be expected, and the shares of social-insurance contributions and indirect business taxes moving countercyclically (in considering these results, recall that an increase in the share of one program must be reflected in a decrease in the shares of one or more other programs). The responses are rather strong, with, for example, a one-point rise in the unemployment rate being associated with a reduction of 0.76 percentage points in the personal-income-tax share. It is noteworthy that, according to these figures, the cyclically rooted changes in the personal-income tax and social-insurance contribution shares offset each other almost exactly.

Somewhat surprisingly, neither personal nor corporate tax-revenue shares show evidence of overindexing. However, the share of social-insurance contributions has a positive and significant price-indexing coefficient, while the indirect business tax share shows evidence of underindexing.

Conclusions

It is apparent from these results that the composition of the federal budget has been predominantly determined by trend factors, though cyclical and price-indexing forces also play some role. These trend forces stand for a complex of social, political, demographic, economic, and other factors which are not investigated or made specific here; but their net result has been steady increases in the share of transfer programs on the expenditure side, and in the share of social insurance and personal-income taxes on the revenue side, of the budget. Beyond the shifts in the relationships already accounted for in the estimates (the Korean War spending acceleration, the introduction of general-revenue sharing, the 1964 tax cut), the regressions show evidence of stability over the period covered, suggesting that the trend and other movements we have disentangled are not of recent origin but have been occurring over the whole postwar period. The composition of the federal budget today is due in large part to the persistence of these factors. And to the extent that they are rooted in the set of fundamental forces mentioned above, they seem quite likely to continue to be felt.

Notes

1. See Alan S. Blinder and Howard Y. Esaki, "Macroeconomic Activity and Income Distribution in the Postwar United States," *The Review of Economics and Statistics* 60 (November 1978): 604–609.

2. For an analysis of indexing in the federal budget, see Peter K. Clark, "The Effects of Inflation on Federal Expenditures," background paper no. 9, Congressional Budget Office, Washington, D.C., 1976.

3. Though the size of the budget certainly affects the level of U, it is assumed here that the budget's composition does not have strong enough effects on the unemployment rate to cause serious statistical problems.

4. Note that in 1951 these three programs had declined to 27.4 percent of total budget expenditures, and the upward trend really began from that point.

3 Inflation, Progressivity, and State Income-Tax Revenues

Peter Formuzis and
Anil Puri

In a recent article, Robert Gordon advanced the hypothesis that there exists a "legitimate" demand for inflation by the public because it represents a form of taxation which may be regarded as a substitute for income, sales, and property taxes as a source of government revenue.[1] Gordon's hypothesis holds that the rate of use of each taxing source is a function of marginal-collection costs, with the optimal tax mix and the optimal rate of inflation occurring at the point where each source has identical marginal costs for raising revenue.

With regard to federal finance, inflation generates government revenue (1) through the process of issuing money, with the resulting inflation imposing a tax on cash balances by depreciating the real quantity of money, and (2) by shifting taxpayers into higher-marginal brackets under the progressive rate system. State governments which have progressive income-tax systems also gain revenue through inflation by the movement of taxpayers into higher brackets. Unlike the federal government, however, they cannot gain through the depreciation of the real-money stock, as that revenue source is restricted only to the issuer of money.

Although both federal and state governments gain revenue through inflation, the existing literature on the subject is entirely dominated by the effects of inflation on federal finance. This is no doubt explained by a number of factors, including the greater magnitude of federal income taxes relative to state income taxes, the relative unimportance or nonexistence of income taxes in several states, and the fact that only the federal government is in the position to capture the revenue associated with the depreciation of the real quantity of money. The neglect of the impact of inflation on state income revenues, however, is surprising in view of the thirty-nine states which have progressive taxes, the growing importance of state income taxes relative to other taxes, and the rapid growth of state expenditures over the past thirty-five years. This study provides some evidence on the relationship between inflation and growth in state income taxes, and develops a more complete understanding of the role played by inflation in financing the subnational public sector.

25

Postwar Growth in State Income-Tax Revenues

Between 1947 and 1977, the ratio of state income taxes to gross national product (GNP) rose 740 percent. Over the same period, federal income-tax revenues relative to GNP showed approximately no change, though there was some variation from year to year. The stability in federal effective tax rates has been a consequence of numerous congressional discretionary tax-code changes over the past thirty years, and has been observed by many others, including Aaron,[2] Goetz and Weber,[3] and Sunley and Pechman[4]. There is no consensus on the underlying reasons why Congress and the presidency acted in this particular fashion, but as a result of de facto indexation, the federal government "gave up" a significant amount of the income-tax revenue from inflation that it might otherwise have received.

State governments, however, did not follow a similar pattern. Instead of reducing statutory rates in the presence of inflation, every state with an income-tax system raised rates at least once, and thirteen states had three or more increases. In terms of relative importance, state income taxes increased from 3 percent of aggregate state revenue in 1946 to 11 percent in 1977[5]. These events indicate that states and not the federal government largely captured the revenues associated with the movement of taxpayers into higher-tax brackets.

In 1978, California became the first state to enact legislation partially indexing the state personal-income tax against inflation. In 1979, legislation was introduced to fully index the tax for a two-year trial period, and a referendum to substantially reduce income-tax rates is on the June 1980 ballot. Other states, too, are adopting different types of tax-limitation measures. In light of these trends, Gordon's hypothesis warrants further examination. While we do not directly test his hypothesis, the evidence presented here is useful to its empirical interpretation.

Inflation and the Growth of State Income-Tax Revenues

The growth in the ratio of state income-tax revenues to personal income may be attributed to five factors: (1) states which imposed income taxes for the first time; (2) those which increased statutory rates; (3) the growth in real income in those states with progressive tax structures; (4) shifts in the composition of factor inputs and outputs; and (5) existence of inflation in states with progressive rates.

In a simplified situation—where there are no increases in statutory rates, no states add income taxes, and all income-tax structures are proportional—the ratio of the aggregate of state income-tax revenues to personal income would be reasonably constant. An empirical test of this hypothesis may be made by examining tax to personal income ratios in those states which had proportional tax systems and which did not change statutory rates over some period. These restrictions place strong limitations on the time periods available for analysis. The periods 1960–1966, 1966–1970, and 1970–1974 and the states of Connecticut, Illinois, Tennessee, and New Hampshire are considered here because the time periods and the states chosen meet both conditions.

Table 3–1 records the annualized percentage increase in the ratio of income tax to personal income, together with the annual rates of inflation taken from the consumer price index (CPI). The results show a small increase in the income-tax ratios in each subperiod, but no apparent correspondence to the movements in the rate of inflation. The disparity between the hypothesized zero growth of the ratio and the actual figures may be accounted for by the presence of exemptions and credits which introduce some progressivity into tax systems with proportional rates, changes in the composition of output and factor payments, tax-code changes other than rates, and the administration of tax assessments and collections.

By way of comparison, table 3–2 shows the ratio of income tax to personal income for states with progressive statutory rates over the same periods used in table 3–1. The states were restricted to those which did not increase rates in each of the subperiods (Alabama, Colorado, Georgia, Hawaii, Kansas, Kentucky, Louisiana, North Carolina, and South Carolina).

The results for these states show annualized rates of increase in the ratios of tax to personal income which are substantially above those for the proportional rate states. In particular, these figures indicate that the absolute increase in income-tax revenues exceeded the increase in personal income for these states. The results also reveal a direct relationship between the rate of growth in the ratio and the rate of inflation in each subperiod.

Table 3–1
Income-Tax Collections in Proportional Rate States and the Rate of Inflation

Years	Annual Percentage Increase in Ratio of Tax to Personal Income	Annual Percentage Rate of Inflation
1960–1966	1.12	1.53
1966–1970	0.62	4.09
1970–1974	1.39	6.15
1960–1974	1.06	3.71

As in the case of the proportional rate states, the changes in revenues shown in table 3-2 are a product of changes in the composition of output, factor payments, and tax administration, plus an added increment related to the rate of inflation and real-income growth. To what extent is the rise in the ratio of income taxes to personal income related to inflation? This is a difficult question to answer with any precision from the aggregate data presented here. A preliminary measure, however, is possible.

In principle, inflation and real-income growth of equal magnitude should have the same impact on the ratio of income tax to personal income. Accordingly, the sum of the percentage rates of inflation and real-income growth should be related to the annual rate of increase in the ratio of income tax to personal income, with the proportion of the increase due to inflation expressed as the ratio of the inflation rate to the sum of the rates of real growth and inflation. Taking the rates of growth in real GNP as the real-growth index, the corresponding percentages of the increase in the ratios of income taxes to personal income due to inflation shown in table 3-2 are 23 percent between 1960 and 1966; 56 percent between 1966 and 1970; 57 percent between 1970 and 1974; and 47 percent for the full period 1960-1974.

Inflation and the Relative Share of Income Tax in General Revenue

Over the postwar period, there have been substantial changes in the composition of total state and local revenue. Table 3-3 records these shifts over the period 1946-1977. The figures are the result of many economic and institutional changes that occurred over this time span and cannot be attributed to a single factor. However, inflation and real-income growth in those states with progressive rates would be expected to contribute toward an increase in the share of income taxes in total general revenue.

To determine what if any relationship exists between changes in the relative share of income taxes and inflation, the rate of real growth and the degree of progressivity of the income tax must also be taken into account. Assuming that the rate of real-income growth varies from state to state while the rate of inflation is constant for all states, changes in the share of income taxes in general revenue can be expressed as a function of the degree of progressivity and the rate of real-income growth. Accordingly, the following relationship is specified:

$$\Delta t = f(d, g)$$

where Δt = percentage change in the ratio of income taxes to total revenue,

Table 3-2
Income-Tax Collections in Progressive Rate States and the Rate of Inflation

Years	Annual Percentage Increase in Ratio of Tax to Personal Income	Annual Percentage Rate of Inflation
1960–1966	3.59	1.53
1966–1970	5.29	4.09
1970–1974	6.08	6.15
1960–1974	4.78	3.71

Table 3-3
Percentage of State and Local Revenue Sources to Total State and Local Revenue, 1946–1977

Revenue Source	Percentage of Total Revenue	
	1946	1977
State income taxes	3	11
Property taxes	44	23
Sales taxes	26	23
Federal grants	10	25
Other	17	18
Total	100	100

d = index of the degree of income-tax progressivity, and g = percentage rate of real-personal-income growth. This particular specification implies that in a linear regression equation the constant term will measure, among other things, the effect of inflation.[6]

Data from thirty-six states for the period 1971–1975 were used in the analysis. The states comprised those which had income-tax systems at the beginning and end of the period and which held statutory rates constant. The progressivity index, d, was constructed by taking the ratio of income tax of a high-income household to that of a low-income household in each state. A high-income household was defined as one with a family income twice that of the average family and a low-income household, 75 percent of that of the average family. The percentage rate of real-income growth, g, was taken as the percentage increase in each state's per capita personal income deflated by the CPI.

The linear regression result for the cross section of thirty-six states yielded

$$\Delta t = -290.4 + 9.7d + 47.2g \qquad \bar{R}^2 = .61$$
$$(-81.3) \quad (1.5) \quad (14.6)$$

where the terms in the parentheses are the standard errors of the estimated coefficients. The results indicate that both the degree of progressivity and the rate of real-income growth are statistically significant at the 1-percent level, with higher degrees of tax system progressivity and real-income growth associated with higher-percentage increases in the ratio of income taxes to general revenue.

Summary

The evidence presented here indicates that the combination of progressivity and inflation has had significant impacts on state income-tax collections. First, the ratio of income taxes to personal income has grown significantly more in states with progressive income taxes than those with proportional rate structures. The rate of inflation was found to be responsible for roughly half of that growth. Second, inflation appears to have affected income-tax revenues to a greater extent than other sources of states and local revenue. The degree of tax progressivity together with real rates of income growth are the main determinants of this impact.

Although the income tax is not the most important source of state and local revenue, the current inflationary environment has increased its role in the overall revenue picture. This increase in the relative position of the income tax has, however, stimulated recent resistance in some states which have installed income-tax indexation measures and considered income-tax-rate rollbacks or other measures designed to reduce the relative importance of income taxes in total collections.

Finally, it is interesting to note that the two sources of government revenue generated by inflation have been split between the federal and state governments. The federal government has de facto indexed the federal personal-income tax since 1950 and has largely limited its gain from inflation to those associated with the issuance of money and the corresponding depreciation of the real quantity of money. State governments with progressive income-tax systems, on the other hand, have generally increased their statutory rates in the presence of inflation, thereby capturing considerable additional revenue. It is *as if* the federal government created an automatic revenue source for the majority of states to assist them in paying for federally mandated programs over the years. Inflation has been a significant factor influencing the growth in state and local expenditures in the postwar period.

Notes

1. Robert J. Gordon, "The Demand and Supply of Inflation," *Journal of Law and Economics* (December 1975):807–836.

2. Henry Aaron, "Inflation and the Income Tax," *American Economic Review* (May 1976):193–199.

3. Charles J. Goetz and Warren E. Weber, "Intertemporal Changes in Real Federal Income Tax Rates, 1954-1970," *National Tax Journal* (March 1971):51–63.

4. Emil M. Sunley and Joseph A. Pechman, "Inflation Adjustment for the Individual Income Tax," in Henry J. Aaron, ed., *Inflation and the Income Tax* (Washington D.C., Brookings, 1976).

5. All the tax and income data for individual states were taken from various issues of *Facts and Figures on Government Finance,* Tax Foundation, Inc.

6. In an alternative specification where the rate of inflation varies across states or one is dealing with time-series data, the rate of inflation would be included as a separate explanatory variable.

Part II
Causes of Growth in
Public Spending

4 State-Revenue Elasticity and Expenditure Growth

Susan B. Hansen and
Patrick Cooper

The purpose here is to assess the contribution of elasticity of tax revenues to the growth in American state expenditures since 1960. The income elasticity of revenue flow measures the sensitivity of a government's tax system to changes in personal income. A highly elastic revenue system can generate considerable additional tax monies even if no changes are made in the tax rate or base. As a fiscal illusion (Buchanan 1967; Goetz 1977), revenue elasticity should therefore contribute to growth in government expenditures. Insofar as revenues can increase without any politically hazardous actions such as new tax legislation, "taxpayer consciousness and hence subjective tax burden would be minimized" (Goetz 1977:176).

This theory is supported by some evidence from the American states. Penniman (1976) noted faster rates of increase in expenditures in states which rely primarily on income taxes than in sales-tax states, the latter presumably having less elastic revenue systems. Goetz (1977:n6, p. 184) noted a positive coefficient for the income elasticity of state-revenue systems in a regression equation predicting determinants of state general revenue during the 1960s. However, these analyses cover a limited time period. In Penniman's analysis, only sixteen states were involved, and her comparison of sales-tax and income-tax states does not measure differences in elasticity across all states or for the total tax system in any state. These studies also fail to control for other factors which might also account for increases in state spending. Economic growth is one such factor since demand for public services and capacity to pay for them are presumed to increase with personal income. Population growth is another factor because of the demands it places on existing facilities and services. Intergovernmental aid is a third factor; recent empirical evidence summarized in Gramlich (1977) suggested that 25 to 50 percent of the growth in state and local spending can be attributed to the stimulation of federal grants of various types. Even if federal grants have encouraged state spending by requiring matching funds for many categories of expenditures, states have still had to find ways to generate that additional revenue. Nor can one ignore the propensities of bureaucrats and politicians—at least before the passage of California's Proposition 13—to seek larger budgets for the public sector.

Our task here is to determine whether state-revenue elasticity has had any impact on the recent growth in state spending from 3.8 percent of gross national product (GNP) in 1960 to 6.8 percent of GNP by 1975. For this purpose, we will consider time-series data on state revenues, expenditures, social and political characteristics, and legislative changes in tax rates and tax bases for the period 1960–1976. We first test whether the overall relationship between state-revenue growth and elasticity is positive as hypothesized, and whether this relationship is monotonic or variable according to the degree of elasticity, level of spending, or time period. We next assess the independent contribution (as measured by regression coefficients) of elasticity and tax-structure changes once we introduce controls for other growth factors: population, income, and federal grants to the states. Finally, we consider some reasons why states have varied in their propensity to adopt elastic revenue structures.

Data and Measurement

Revenue elasticity is a product of two factors: first, changes in state tax structures over time; and second, the income elasticity of various types of state taxes weighted by their contribution to total revenue. Over time, revenue elasticity may change considerably due to changes in legislation as well as in the composition of state personal income and consumption.

The time period we have selected, 1960 through 1976, involved considerable growth in state revenues, expenditures, and federal aid to states. We used Burkhead's (1963) estimates of revenue elasticity for 1950–1960 to rank the states as of 1960. The Advisory Commission on Intergovernmental Relations provided estimates of revenue elasticity for 1968 and 1970 (ACIR 1969, 1971) based on individual income, general sales, and selected sales taxes by state. Although the ACIR recently computed changes in state revenues due to legislative actions and economic growth (ACIR 1976–1977), this is not available by state for each year. For an estimate of legislative effects on revenues, we use an index computed by Condon (1976). This assigns each state a revenue-structure index of 1.0 in 1950 (the base year) and computes changes in this index due to legislative action for each year through 1971; we used her figures for 1960 and 1971.

Our dependent variables are the percentage changes in state total general expenditures for 1960–1970, 1970–1976, and 1960–1976 (U.S. Bureau of the Census, *Compendium of State Government Finance,* various years). Population changes for these three periods are taken from the census of population. The growth in state personal income is from the U.S. Department of Commerce, *Survey of Current Business,* various years. The percentage change in state own-source revenue and in federal aid to state governments is also taken from the *Compendium of State Government Finance.*

Results

Table 4-1 shows Pearson correlations between rates of change in state revenues and expenditures and our measures of revenue elasticity and legislative changes in tax structure. The correlations are positive for 1960-1970 and 1960-1976 for both revenues and expenditures paired with measures of revenue elasticity. But the correlations are far from robust and the signs are *negative* for 1970-1976. Further, examination of scatterplots showed that the positive correlation of .15 between 1970 revenue elasticity (ACIR measure) and expenditure growth 1960-1976 was due to one significant outlier (Alaska); if this deviant case was excluded, the correlation for the other forty-nine states became weak and negative ($R = -.08$). The elimination of Alaska also reduced the correlations for 1960-1970 and 1970-1976. Clearly, differences in expenditure increases across states must depend on factors other than revenue elasticity.

Condon's (1976) estimates of legislative effects on state-revenue structures showed somewhat stronger correlations with changes in revenues and expenditures. Changes in legislation (the difference between her 1960 and

Table 4-1
Revenue Elasticity, Legislative Actions, and Changes in State Revenues and Expenditures, 1960-1976

	Percentage of Change in State Revenues			Percentage of Change in State Expenditures		
	1960-1970	*1970-1976*	*1960-1976*	*1960-1970*	*1970-1976*	*1960-1976*
Correlations with revenue elasticity						
1950-1960 [a]	0.08	-0.01	0.13	0.15	-0.02	0.15
1968 estimate [b]	0.08	0.11	0.09	0.07	-0.07	0.03
1970 estimate [c]	0.13	0.11	0.14	0.10	-0.07	0.05
Correlations with legislative actions [d]						
LE 1960	0.23	0.09	0.29	0.27	0.15	0.31
LE 1971	0.45	0.20	0.48	0.46	0.12	0.47
Change in legislative effects, 1960-1971	0.47	0.20	0.47	0.44	0.06	0.43

[a] Jesse Burkhead, *State and Local Taxes for Public Education* (Syracuse University Press, 1963), p. 90.

[b] Advisory Commission on Intergovernmental Relations, *State and Local Finances: Significant Features 1967 to 1970* (Washington, D.C.: 1969) table 27, p. 67.

[c] Advisory Commission on Intergovernmental Relations, *Significant Features of Fiscal Federalism 1976-1977*, 2 (Washington, D.C.: 1977), table 32.

[d] Carol M. Condon, "Fluctuations in Tax Collections of Individual States, (Ph.D. diss. Columbia University, 1978), table 2, pp. 19 ff.

1971 measures) also showed fairly strong correlations with taxing and spending changes, at least for the 1960–1970 period.

One should note that these measures of revenue elasticity and legislative effects are largely independent of one another. Although Condon's 1971 index was highly correlated ($R = .70$) with her 1960 index, both measures showed negative correlations with the ACIR's estimates of revenue elasticity. States with high-income elasticity of revenues in 1960 were less likely to alter their tax structures as much as states with less elastic sources. But most states did make considerable changes in their revenue structures, including new taxes as well as rate increases or base extensions, during the 1960s. Thus the ranking of states by elasticity in 1950–1960 (Burkhead) showed a modest Spearman Rho (.13) to elasticity rankings by 1971 (ACIR). We therefore found it necessary to run separate regressions to indicate the impact of different elasticities on changes in state expenditures over time.

The next phase of our analysis was the regression of state-expenditure percentage increases on the various tax-structure measures, controlling for changes in state personal income, population, and federal aid. For the periods 1960–1970 and 1960–1976, the partials for revenue elasticity remain positive but even weaker than the simple correlations suggested. Changes in federal grants to states appeared to be the major factor accounting for state-expenditure growth, with regression coefficients ranging from 2.81 (1970–1976) to 4.36 (1960–1976). Population growth also had a strong impact on changes in state-spending patterns, especially among fast-growing states in the sunbelt. But the impact of population change was not symmetrical, since even states which declined in population showed increases in expenditures.

For the period 1970–1976, however, the sign of the regression coefficient for revenue elasticity (ACIR 1976–1977) is weakly *negative* (equation 1, table 4–2). Once the factors are introduced into the equation, states with highly elastic revenue systems showed slower rates of growth in expenditures than states with inelastic revenue structures.

Why this puzzling reversal of the predictions of public finance? The major reason appears to be that states with highly elastic revenue systems may have had too much of a good thing. By the mid-1970s, several states (Wisconsin, California, Minnesota) had amassed sizable surpluses. The excess of revenues over expenditures totaled across all states was so large ($18 billion in FY 1976, $29 billion in FY 1977) that the Council of Economic Advisers advocated an increased federal deficit to offset the "fiscal drag" exerted by these surpluses in an economy just emerging from recession. In several states, politicians preferred cutting taxes to increasing expenditures; Michigan, highly vulnerable to recessions, put revenue surpluses into a rainy-day fund to meet future contingencies. Penniman's (1976) case study of Governor Lucey's handling of Wisconsin's budget

Table 4-2
Regression Coefficients for Prediction of Increases in State Expenditures, 1960–1976

Percentage of Change in State Expenditures	Tax Structure B_1	Percentage of Change Personal Income B_2	Percentage of Change Population B_3	Percentage of Change Federal Aid B_4	Constant C	Variance Explained R^2
1970–1976						
1. B_1 = 1970 revenue elasticity	−.12 (1.5)	.12 (.08)	1.14* (.36)	3.50* (.60)	.53 (.15)	.51
2. B_1 = legislative effects, 1971	.00 (.00)	.01 (.08)	1.11* (.34)	2.81* (.63)	.50 (.14)	.41
1960–1970						
3. B_1 = 1968 revenue elasticity (ACIR)	.012* (.00)	−.14 (.18)	1.39 (.70)	3.9* (1.3)	−.21 (.61)	.36
4. B_1 = 1960 revenue elasticity (Burkhead)	.002 (.003)	.11 (.12)	.98* (.47)	3.6* (.47)	1.71 (.53)	.63
5. B_1 = legislative effects, 1960	.003 (.03)	.004 (.09)	.31 (.35)	4.1* (.60)	.53 (.32)	.58
1960–1976						
6. B_1 = 1960 revenue elasticity (Burkhead)	.02 (.002)	.10 (.12)	.98* (.47)	3.58* (.48)	1.74 (.53)	.63
7. B_1 = 1968 revenue elasticity (ACIR)	.029 (.02)	.35 (.33)	2.54* (1.32)	4.36* (1.36)	−2.13 (1.77)	.39
8. B_1 = 1960 legislative effects	.008 (.006)	.02 (.07)	1.00* (.44)	3.41* (.49)	1.38 (.65)	.63
9. B_1 = change in legislative effects, 1960–1971 (Condon)	.00 (.00)	.05 (.09)	1.13* (.36)	2.9* (.06)	.42 (.14)	.43

*Starred coefficients are at least twice their standard errors.

surplus showed that, given an elastic tax structure and good economic conditions, states can generate more income than their governments can absorb (at least in the short run), and find other alternatives more politically profitable and economically feasible than increasing expenditures.

We considered and rejected two alternative explanations for this negative relationship between growth and revenue elasticity. Federal aid does not flow disproportionately to states with the least-elastic revenue systems; in fact, the correlation between federal aid and elasticity (ACIR) was .08 for the 1960s and .20 for the 1970s. Nor did states which adopted income taxes since 1970 account for this pattern; these states were not among the significant outliers from the regression line, and a dummy variable for recent income-tax adoption had little effect on equation 1. It appears that the relationship between revenue elasticity and state spending is monotonic and increasing *within limits.* The budgets and the taxpayers of several states may have reached those limits during the 1970s.

Although Condon's index of legislative tax changes continued to show a positive association with changes in expenditures, the regression coefficients were markedly lower than the simple correlations reported in table 4-1, and contributed little to the explained variance. Even the change in legislative effects (equation 9 in table 4-2) had little net impact on expenditures. Federal aid to states has had a far greater impact on state spending than have efforts by states to increase revenue from their own sources, even in states which have made considerable changes in their tax structures since 1960.

Discussion

If revenue elasticity has so little effect on state spending once other factors are controlled, why do some states have more highly elastic tax structures than others? And which states have changed their tax structures since 1960?

Answers to these questions are quite different before and after 1960 or so. The earliest states to adopt income taxes tended to have the most elastic tax structures up through the early 1960s. One would have to look at conditions in those states at the time of initial tax adoptions to account for this pattern. Such analysis is beyond the scope of this study, but as Hansen (1978) has shown, less competitive states tended to be innovators of broad-based taxes, and such taxes were adopted in more competitive states only under conditions which reduced the political threat to the party initiating them: realigning elections or control of the state's executive and legislature by the same political party. Politicians in more competitive states have historically been more sympathetic to highly elastic tax structures, which permitted steady increases in revenues without the political hazards involved in implementing new taxes.

In recent years, however, the picture has changed. As demands for state revenues have increased, states with the least-elastic tax structures have been under the most pressure to revise their revenue systems. After 1960, we find that the least competitive states have made the greatest amount of legislative changes in their taxes. The current relationship between competition and elasticity is *negative* ($R = -.29$) with Ranney's (1976) index of party competition for 1960–1973 and $R = -.35$ with the percentage of one-party governments in an state, 1960–1976. As of 1960, however, the correlation between competition and elasticity (Burkhead) or legislative effects (Condon) was positive, with R's of .17 and .3, respectively. The less competitive states have therefore had both the need and the political capacity to generate additional revenues.

Both taxing and spending have increased considerably in the American states since 1960. Revenue elasticity, however, has had little to do with this change. Instead, as most taxpayers are painfully aware, tax rates have increased markedly. Seventeen states have adopted new sales or income taxes, while many others have expanded the tax base. The major effects of these changes has been to permit states to keep abreast of demands for higher expenditures posed by population growth and rising personal income; our analysis shows that revenue elasticity had only a moderate impact on state spending in the 1960s and no effect in the 1970s, where tax cutting has become the norm in many of the states with the highest-revenue elasticities.

Our analysis should not be construed to indicate that "fiscal illusions" have played no part in the growth in state expenditures. A major factor underlying state-spending increases appears to be increased federal aid to states. The growth here has been possible at least in part because of the high-revenue elasticity of the progressive federal income tax and because (as critics of revenue-sharing claim) the linkage between revenue and expenditures is weak when the federal government foots the bills for expanded state services.

References

Advisory Commission on Intergovernmental Relations, *Significant Features of Fiscal Federalism,* 1967–1970, 1968–1971, 1976–1977 (Washington, D.C.: 1969, 1971, 1977).

Buchanan, James M. *Public Finance in Democratic Process* (Chapel Hill, N.C.: University of North Carolina Press, 1967).

Burkhead, Jesse, *State and Local Taxes for Public Education* (Syracuse, N.Y.: Syracuse University Press, 1963).

Condon, Carol M., "Fluctuations in Tax Collections of Individual States" Ph.D. diss., (Columbia University, 1976).

Goetz, Charles J., "Fiscal Illusion in State and Local Finance," in *Budgets and Bureaucrats,* ed. Thomas Borcherding, (Durham, N.C.: Duke University Press, 1977).

Gramlich, Edward M., "Intergovernmental Grants: A Review of the Empirical Literature," in *Fiscal Federalism,* ed. Wallace Oates, (Lexington, Mass.: Lexington Books, D.C. Heath and Co., 1977).

Hansen, Susan B., "The Politics of State Tax Innovation" (paper presented at the Midwest Political Science Association, Chicago, April, 1978).

Penniman, Clara, "The Politics of Taxation," in *Politics in the American States,* ed Herbert Jacob and Kenneth M. Vines, 3d ed. (Boston: Little, Brown, 1976), pp. 428–464.

Ranney, Austin, "Parties in the American States," in *Politics in the American States,* ed. Herbert Jacob and Kenneth M. Vines, (Boston: Little, Brown, 1976), pp. 51–92.

5

Urban Riots and the Growth of State-Welfare Expenditures

Edward T. Jennings, Jr.

This chapter examines the relationship between the urban riots of the 1960s and increases in state-welfare spending. The findings suggest that riots had little independent influence on state-welfare-spending increases from own-source funds, but that the riots may have influenced state-welfare-spending increases financed with federal grants. These relationships are explored and some possible causal relationships are mapped. The findings are tentative because of the state of research, limitations of the data set, and unresolved questions.

During the period 1964–1971, the American states increased welfare spending from combined federal and state funds by a startling 209 percent. The increase in welfare spending from state funds alone averaged 227 percent. Of additional interest is the fact that increases in welfare spending were so variable among the states, ranging from 46 percent in Louisiana to 545 percent in New Jersey. Eight states increased welfare expenditures by less than 100 percent; in eleven, the increase was more than 300 percent. During the same period, the average increase in general state expenditures was only 132 percent. The variability of increases in general expenditures was also much less than the variability of increases in welfare spending. The coefficient of variation for welfare spending increases was 51 percent; for general expenditures, it was 26 percent.

One possible explanation for the sharp, variable increases in state-welfare spending is the urban rioting which occurred during the same period. Although scholars have differed greatly in their understanding of the evidence, most popular and scholarly interpretations of the riots locate their origins in the economic, social, and political problems of urban blacks in America.[1] The major officially sponsored study of the riots placed a great deal of importance on such problems.[2] Given such explanations for the urban riots, one might expect public officials to have responded with expanded welfare services designed to alleviate the problems involved. Extending welfare benefits to large numbers of recipients and raising benefit levels might have served to reduce frustration, deprivation, and anger, while providing government officials with greater control over portions of the black community.

Frances Piven and Richard Cloward theorized in a provocative analysis, in fact, that the welfare system functions as a mechanism of social control.[3] In their view, welfare rolls are restricted and benefit levels are kept low during periods of social quiescence in order to ensure a supply of low-wage labor. During periods of civil disorder rooted in economic dis-locations, the rolls are expanded as a means of placating and controlling rebellious elements of the population. Thus, welfare policy is a mechanism whereby social control is maintained. Piven and Cloward did not focus directly on the question of welfare expenditures. They dealt much more specifically with the growth of welfare rolls. A logical corollary of their theory, however, is that welfare spending would also increase in response to civil turmoil.

These considerations lead to the proposition that urban riots and wel-fare-spending increases in the 1960s were related. This possibility can be tested using states as the units of analysis. If the riots were a major cause of expanded welfare budgets, then variations in state-welfare-spending increases should be explained, at least in part, by variations in the number of urban riots among the states.

Although the riots were an urban phenomenon which occurred generally within municipal jurisdictions, welfare policy in America has been, in many respects, principally the responsibility of state governments. It is states which establish criteria of eligibility, set benefit levels, and determine administrative practices for the categorical assistance programs. Although the national government has generally determined the categories of public assistance and placed constraints on state policy through welfare grant provisions of the Social Security Act, states have remained free to set their own spending levels. The independence of state policy is reflected in the varying recipient rates, benefit levels, and expenditures of the states. Local governments, though frequently having administrative functions, have little financial responsibility in general for welfare programs.

Analysis

The analysis focuses on the relationship between changes in welfare expen-ditures from fiscal year 1964 to fiscal year 1971 and the number of riots which occurred in each state during that period. These years encompass the period when civil turmoil ravaged the cities.

Two measures of welfare-expenditure change provide the focus of the analysis. One is the percentage change in state-welfare expenditures, net of federal assistance. The other is percentage change in state-welfare expendi-tures from federal funds. Although it has been suggested that federal wel-fare grants are a direct determinant of state-welfare expenditures, there are reasons to question such an assertion.[4] In the first place, states can be highly successful at manipulating federal social-service grants. In the second place, federal support for categorical aid programs is awarded to states according to a formula which relies heavily on state-spending levels. Thus, one could argue that the amount of federal funding received by a state is a product of state decisions, including those on welfare budgets. Separating expenditures from these two sources of funds, as is done here, opens some interesting avenues of inquiry.

The many comparative studies of state politics and policies suggest a number of other variables for inclusion in the analysis. Among those considered here are indicators of socioeconomic development, such as per capita income; change in per capita income, percentage metropolitan, and percentage of the population below the poverty line; the closeness of interparty competition, as an indicator of one feature of the political system; and community action agency (CAA) expenditures per poor person from 1964 to 1970. CAA expenditures are considered because of Piven and Cloward's contention that these programs promoted expansion of the welfare rolls.

Coefficients for bivariate correlations, reported in table 5-1, present some interesting findings. The first is that increases in welfare spending are related to the number of riots in the states; however, the relationship is moderate and it is significantly stronger for spending from federal grants than for spending from the states' own resouces. The strongest relationships

Table 5-1

The Relationship of Welfare Spending Change Measures and the Number of Urban Riots to Each Other and to Measures of Socioeconomic Development and Politics, American States, 1964-1971

	Number of Riots	Percentage of Change in Welfare Spending from State Funds	Percentage of Change in Welfare Spending from Federal Funds
Number of riots	1.00	0.30	0.47
Percentage of change in welfare spending, state funds	0.30	1.00	0.61
Percentage of change in welfare spending, federal funds	0.47	0.61	1.00
Percentage metropolitan	0.59	0.37	0.51
Per capita income	0.47	0.42	0.62
Percentage in poverty	−0.29	−0.30	−0.50
CAA expenditure per poor person	0.09	0.21	0.11
Percentage of change in per capita income	−0.15	−0.15	−0.38
Interparty competition	0.22	0.16	0.36

are those between per capita personal income and welfare-expenditure increases and percentage metropolitan and expenditure increases, findings which are consistent with those of a number of studies of state expenditures. Percentage increase in per capita income and percentage poor are negatively related to spending increases. As one would expect, percentage increase in federally funded spending is strongly, but far from perfectly, related to percentage increase in state-funded welfare spending. CAA spending is weakly related to riots and spending increases.

Perhaps the most important finding is that the increase in welfare spending from federal funds is consistently more strongly related to the independent variables than is the increase from state funds. This pattern of relationships may reflect one of two things: (1) an increased effort on the part of riot states to obtain federal social-welfare grants; (2) efforts by the federal government to target grants at the states which experienced the most severe turmoil.

Of these two explanations, the first seems more likely. The bulk of federal welfare aid to the states comes in the form of grants for the categorical assistance programs, such as Aid to Families with Dependent Children [and Old Age Assistance (OAA), Aid to the Blind (AB), and Aid to the Permanently and Totally Disabled (APTD) during the period under consideration]. If anything, federal grant formulas for these programs were shifting during the 1960s in directions beneficial to states with low per capita incomes and large populations of poor people. States with low per capita incomes began to receive higher matching grants, proportionately, and a higher proportion of low average grants was covered by federal aid. The finding that percentage change in federal aid was strongly and positively related to per capita income contrasts sharply with these federal policy changes.

Also of note in table 5-1 is the finding that need for welfare services, as reflected by percentage poor, was negatively related to increases in welfare spending. This may reflect an inability of poor states to meet the needs of their poor residents, since the association between per capita income and percentage poor is negative and high ($R = -.84$); however, it may also reflect improving opportunities for the poor to be self-sufficient, since percentage change in per capita income has a strong positive association with percentage poor.

Table 5-2 presents partial correlations between percentage change in welfare expenditures and riots, while controlling for other variables. The relationship between rioting and welfare-spending changes financed with state funds is virtually eliminated when per capita income or percentage metropolitan is controlled.

On the other hand, controlling for rioting in table 5-3 reduces, but does not eliminate, the relationship of income and percentage metropolitan to

Table 5-2
Partial Correlations between Riots and Welfare-Spending Change

Control Variables	Partial Correlation between Riots and Percentage Change in Welfare Spending, State Funds	Partial Correlation between Riots and Percentage Change in Welfare Spending, Federal Funds
Income	.13	.26
Metro	.11	.25
IPC	.28	.43
Poverty	.23	.39

Table 5-3
Partial Correlations of Welfare-Spending Change Measures with Four Independent Variables, Controlling for Number of Riots

Independent Variables	Percentage Change in Welfare Spending, State Funds	Percentage Change in Welfare Spending, Federal Funds
Income	0.33	0.55
Metropolitan	0.25	0.33
IPC	0.10	0.29
Poverty	-0.23	-0.43

changes in spending from state funds. At the same time, the relationship and changes in spending from federal funds remains fairly significant when other variables are controlled. Variables such as income and percentage metropolitan are moderately to strongly related to changes in spending from federal funds when controlling for riots.

All of this suggests that rioting had little independent impact on welfare-expenditure increases from state funds, but that both riots and standard variables from the literature contribute to an explanation for increased expenditures from federal funds. This finding is confirmed in a series of regression equations not presented here. Rioting adds little to the explained variance in a set of three variable equations relating income and percentage metropolitan to changes in welfare spending from state funds. It does contribute to the explained variance in equations with change in welfare spending from federal funds as the dependent variable.

As a final step of the current analysis, the effect of income, percentage metropolitan, percentage poor, interparty competition, and riots was estimated with a stepwise regression technique, which entered variables in terms of their contribution to variance explained and omitted all variables with an F ratio of less than 1.0. With percentage change in welfare spending from state funds as the dependent variable, the following result was obtained (standard errors in parentheses):

$$Y = -82.44 + .101 \text{ Income} + 1.12 \text{ Metropolitan}$$
$$(.053) \qquad\qquad (.90)$$

The equation explains 20 percent of the variance. Of that, 17.5 percent is explained by per capita income.

With percentage change in state-welfare spending from federal funds as the dependent variable, the following result was obtained:

$$Y = -101.46 + .120 \text{ Income} + 1.77 \text{ Riots}$$
$$(.030) \qquad\qquad (.97)$$

This equation explains 42 percent of the variance; income alone explains 38 percent of the variance.

Several things stand out. First, in terms of spending from state funds, only the standard socioeconomic development measures contribute independently to the explanation of variance. The effect of riots, if it exists, is obscured by the importance of wealth and urbanization. In terms of spending from federal funds, only income and rioting contribute independently to the explanation of variance.

Conclusion

The findings of this research suggest that urban riots did not have a substantial impact on state-welfare-spending increases, though they may have influenced increased spending from federal grants. If the search for federal money caused states to increase their own expenditures, then riots may have indirectly influenced the growth of spending from state funds. Of additional relevance to the Piven-Cloward thesis is the fact that there is little evidence that spending for community action had much impact on state-welfare spending.

There are a large number of unresolved questions. The variables employed in this analysis leave a substantial amount of the variance unexplained. There is clearly a need for alternative explanations and additional factors to be considered. It is entirely possible that we can obtain a better understanding by looking at the characteristics of party systems, governors, legislatures, public opinion, and electoral processes in the states. We may also need to look more closely at changing population characteristics.

One line of research which may prove fruitful would be to disaggregate welfare spending into various program components at the state level. I have suggested that the findings presented here run counter to what one would expect on the basis of changes in federal funding formulas for public assistance. It is possible, however, that federal funding for other aspects of state-welfare policy developed in a manner that would more than offset the public assistance formulas. Disaggregation may help us come to an understanding of why riots are independently related to increases in welfare spending from federal funds but not to increased spending from state funds.

Notes

1. Academic dispute is reflected in the sharp exchange between Abraham Miller et al. and J. Clarence Davies. See Abraham Miller, Louis Bolce, and Mark Halligan, "The J-Curve Theory and the Black Urban Riots: An Empirical Test of Progressive Relative Deprivation Theory," *American Political Science Review* 71 (September 1977):964–982; idem, "Communication," *American Political Science Review* 72 (December 1978):1358–1360; and J. Clarence Davies, "Communication," *American Political Science Review* 72 (December 1978):1357–1358.

2. National Advisory Commission on Civil Disorders, *Report* (New York: Bantam Books, 1968).

3. Frances Fox Piven and Richard Cloward, *Regulating the Poor: The Functions of Public Welfare* (New York: Vintage Books, Random House, 1971).

4. Among those making this suggestion are Seymour Sacks and Robert Hanis, "The Determinants of State and Local Government Expenditures and the Intergovernmental Flow of Funds," *National Tax Journal* 17 (March 1964):75–85, and James C. Strouse and Philippe Jones, "Federal Aid: The Forgotten Variable in State Policy Research," *Journal of Politics* 36 (February 1974):200–207.

6

A Note on the Political Expenditure Cycle in Latin America

Barry Ames

It is now common in industrialized nations to talk of the political business cycle, that is, an economic cycle reflecting the impact of policies adopted by political leaders primarily to ensure their own survival in office. Though executives in less-industrialized countries often lack the ability to influence macroeconomic outcomes, they are no less interested in retaining office. This chapter is about the strategies adopted by heads of governments in eighteen Latin American countries between 1945 and 1975, with respect to one kind of policy: the allocation of public expenditures. I posit five approaches that executives may choose as they seek to build a coalition capable of staving off military intervention, winning an election, or providing some autonomy in office.[1] Executives adopt one or more of these strategies as a consequence of the sociopolitical conditions they face, including the nature and intensity of cleavages, the strength of barriers to entry by political competitors, the institutional impediments to executive authority, and so on.[2] Each strategy implies particular expenditure programs, and shifts in allocations toward these programs are examined during years of designated as political crises, that is, years in which executives feel heightened insecurity.

Five Strategies for Survival in Latin America

Pacify the Military. Military coups have long been endemic in Latin America. Only Mexico and Nicaragua (*sic*) have not experienced at least one overthrow since 1945. Whether an executive is a civilian or a soldier, the probability of a military coup must be continuously assessed. Coups are more likely when (1) the military has a tradition of intervention, (2) the economy is declining, (3) mass disorder is increasing, (4) the military's financial requests have not been met, and (5) the ideological distance between the executive and the officer corps is great. If the executive judges that a coup is likely, then a direct budgetary reward, that is, an increase in the military's budget share, is one logical response to the soldiers' threat.

This study is an extremely truncated version of my "Survival Strategies and Expenditure Shifts in Latin America." My research has been supported by Washington University, the Tinker Foundation, and Stanford University's Latin American Studies Center.

Recruit Bureaucrats. In Latin America bloated bureaucracies date from colonial times. When the politically relevant population is small (as for example, when indigenous populations are large), public employees and their relatives may constitute important fractions of the population. More-over, public employees are likely to be politically active or linked to activists. To secure the loyalty of a powerful bureaucracy, insecure executives may increase the wage and salary share of the budget.

Reward Territorial Interests. Suppose an important cleavage is geographic. When cleavages are regional or local, and when they manifest themselves in arenas like elections and legislatures, then a suitable response is pork-barrel spending. Public-works expansion, in schools, hospitals, roads, or dams, visibly rewards loyalists and penalizes opposition.

Increase Transfers. Where no intermediate organizations claim rewards, where no strata of activists demand jobs, increases in transfers become the logical medium. Transfer payments retain class selectivity, but the recipient populations are much broader than populations affected by specific programs. A transfer strategy succeeds, for example, when weak political parties occur simultaneously with fiercely competitive leaders. Old parties disappear; new parties form; platforms hardly exist. Followers seem attracted to leaders' personal qualities, their charisma. Groups such as miners, urban workers, or middle-class students may be barely organized but still intensely loyal. To attract their support, pensions increase, social-security benefits grow, more scholarships are awarded.

Reward Social Strata. The social-class cleavages that dominate more advanced countries are at times critically important in Latin America as well, but different regimes seek bases in coalitions of various classes. In a few notable instances (such as Perón in pre-1951 Argentina and Allende in Chile) executives have defended subordinate classes, that is, workers and the urban and rural poor. Multiclass coalitions of middle and working groups are somewhat more common, though such alliances are as difficult to maintain as those based on subordinate elements alone. Reliance on intermediate classes is also possible, with the "reformist" regimes of Frei in Chile and Belaunde in Peru being examples. Finally, dominant classes may react against multiclass or subordinate class coalitions and reverse the gains achieved by the latter. The Brazilian and Chilean military coups of 1964 and 1973 and the establishment of military dictatorships in Argentina and Uruguay represent such authoritarian responses by dominant groups.

Do these various class strategies correspond to particular patterns of public spending? Given the pattern of demands commonly associated with each group, and the class component of the beneficiaries of different programs, we expect subordinate and multiclass strategies to effect increases in health and (to a lesser degree) education spending, intermediate strategies to effect shifts mainly toward education, and dominant strategies to support the repressive forces of military and police.

Measurement and Hypotheses

Which strategy or strategies are optimal for each regime? No easily collectible and rigorous indicators are available for such a coding task, so I relied on a "sophisticated coder" rationale. After an exhaustive search of the monographic literature for each country, I simply decided which strategies seemed optimal and coded dummy variables (one for each strategy) accordingly.[3] It is my belief that most country specialists would regard this task as uncontroversial; indeed, I have checked my coding with specialists whenever possible.

The units of observation (country-years) were partitioned according to whether the year was one of political crisis, that is, a year in which executives would feel maximum insecurity. These typically are the first budgetary year after a military coup or an election, or, if the incumbent or his party compete, the year before an election.

The allocation data analyzed here are final constant-currency expenditures.[4] Focusing on budgetary competition, we are logically interested in shares. Since we predict differential rates of growth, a reasonable conceptualization involves the differences in rates of change of different program pairs. Hence a shift between military (M_t) and public works (PW_t) between years t and $t - 1$ would be

$$\frac{M_t - M_{t-1}}{M_{t-1}} - \frac{PW_t - PW_{t-1}}{PW_{t-1}}$$

In general, the equations I estimate take the form

$$\Delta \text{ military} - \Delta \text{ public works} = A + b(\text{military}) + c(\text{bureaucrats})$$
$$+ d(\text{territorial}) + e(\text{transfers})$$
$$+ f(\text{dominant class}) + g(\text{intermediate})$$
$$+ h(\text{subordinate}) + i(\text{multiclass}) + \mu$$

where Δ military $- \Delta$ public works = the predicted expenditure shift, and $b - i$ = the coefficients associated with dummy variables corresponding to the existence or nonexistence of each strategy. Similar equations with other expenditure trade-offs are estimated, and the data are partitioned into years of political crisis and years in which crises were absent.[5]

Results

Tables 6–1 through 6–5 present abbreviated results for each strategy. The expenditure consequences of military pacification are evident in table 6–1, which demonstrates that during crises programs in health, welfare, police, education, and foreign relations, all lose to the armed forces. The only parameter with the wrong sign comes from the military-transfers trade-off, but this may stem from the serious measurement problems inherent in the transfer data (see below).

Table 6–2 demonstrates that a bureaucratic recruitment strategy leads to an increase in the salary share, but only during crisis. The table also reveals the contrast between bureaucratic and public-works approaches. The latter with a low public-employee wage component, is strongly associated with decreases in the wage share.

Unequivocal results for the territorial interest strategy are provided by table 6–3. All major programs yield to public works when executives pursue this approach. If we apply the model to the same expenditure trade-offs during noncrisis periods, there are no cases in which public works gain at the expense of any other program. The reward of local or regional interests is clearly a strategy pursued for short periods.

The transfer approach proved difficult to test, mostly because governments define transfers inconsistently. Table 6–4 demonstrates simply that when the transfer strategy is optimal and no crisis exists, salaries gain from transfers, but during crisis transfers gain vis-à-vis salaries. In general, however, the data proved inadequate to confirm the existence of a transfer approach.

Table 6–5 presents results for the class strategies. Dominant class reactions lead to military gains against education and health and neutrality (countering a generally negative time trend) in relation to public works and foreign relations; in other words, those programs directly benefiting intermediate and subordinate groups suffer. Intermediate strategies emphasize education—not too surprisingly, given the influence of middle-class teachers and parents. Subordinate and multiclass strategies favor public works and welfare but without penalizing the military. One sees the enormous difficulties faced by such regimes as they try simultaneously to appease the military, stimulate the economy, and provide social benefits. Little wonder they rarely survive.

Table 6-1
Pacification Strategy during the Military Political Crises

Shift to Military from	b^a	$\varrho < /T/^a$	R^{2b}
Health	.1105	.0002	28
Welfare	.0757	.0257	15
Police	.0689	.0014	23
Education	.0305	.1143	17
Public works	.0358	.331	13
Agriculture	.0445	.19	28
Foreign Relations	.0888	.0001	25
Pensions	.0452	.210	73
Transfers	−.1981	.08	15

[a] b and ϱ refer to the coefficient and significance level of the military pacification dummy when all other strategy dummies are included in the equation. For clarity the signs have been reversed, since logs of numbers less than one are negative.

[b] R^2 refers to statistics for the complete regression equations; that is, all strategy dummies are included.

Table 6-2
The Bureaucratic Recruitment Strategy

	Political Crisis		No Political Crisis	
Strategy	b^a	$\varrho < /T/$	b	$\varrho < /T/$
Pacify military	.051	.38	.015	.75
Recruit bureaucrats	.131	.02	−.012	.81
Increase transfers	.037	.63	−.019	.78
Reward territorial interests	−.150	.02	.007	.90
Social strata: dominant classes	−.010	.92	−.015	.85
Social strata: intermediate classes	−.005	.96	.012	.86
Social strata: subordinate classes	−.097	.58	.041	.84
Multiclass	−.012	.88	.019	.82
	$N = 93$	$R^{2b} = 15$	$N = 196$	$R^2 = .06$
	$F = 1.65$	PR $> \varrho = .11$	$F = 1.36$	PR $> \varrho = .21$

Note: Estimation of the share of allocations devoted to salaries in crisis and noncrisis situations.

[a] b and ϱ refer to the coefficient and significance level of the military pacification dummy when all other strategy dummies are included in the equation. For clarity the signs have been reversed, since logs of numbers less than one are negative.

[b] R^2 refers to statistics for the complete regression equations; that is, all strategy dummies are included.

Table 6–3
Tests of the Territorial Interest Strategy during Political Crisis

Shift to Public Works from	b [a]	$\varrho > /T/$	R^2 [b]	N [b]
Military	.110	.007	13	116
Education	.106	.010	8	124
Health	.107	.006	16	71
Foreign relations	.113	.001	11	124
Transfers	.422	.001	70	21
Welfare	.106	.013	15	83
Police	.128	.002	12	122
Agriculture	.102	.044	25	101
Labor	.206	.003	36	35
Pensions	.176	.007	29	48

[a] b and ϱ refer to the coefficients and significance levels of the territorial interest dummy when all other variables are included in the equation.

[b] R^2 and N refer to statistics for the complete regression equation.

Table 6–4
Transfer Strategies

Shift from Transfers to Salaries	b [a]	$\varrho > /T/$	R^2 [b]	N [b]
Condition				
Political crisis	.270	.12	40	21
No political crisis	−.105	.08	14	53

[a] b and ϱ refer to the coefficients and significance levels of the transfer dummy when all other variables are included in the equation.

[b] R and N refer to statistics for the complete regression equation.

Finally, executive decisions about relative shares occur in a context of volatile economic resources. Space limitations prevent more than the comment that trade-offs tend to be largest when the absolute level of total budgetary increase (itself linked to resource increases) is smallest. Hence regimes cushion relative losses by increasing the whole budget enough to prevent absolute declines. This strategy reduces short-run conflict, but its inflationary effects may in the end make regimes' survival continually problematic.

Table 6-5
Social-Class Strategies

Expenditure Trade-off Categories	Estimated Parameter							
	Dominant Classes		Intermediate Classes		Subordinate Classes		Multiclass	
	Noncrisis	Crisis	Noncrisis	Crisis	Noncrisis	Crisis	Noncrisis	Crisis
Education (+) Military (−)	+.024	−.079*	−.013	+.017	+.090*	+.054	+.028	+.051*
Education (+) Public works (+)	−.036	−.037	+.003	+.28	+.014	−.029	+.055*	−.022
Education (+) Foreign relations (−)	−.018	−.048*	−.015	−.011	−.002	+.003	+.021	−.010
Health (+) Military (−)	−.006	−.122*	−.029	−.022	+.075	+.023	+.036	+.029
Health (+) Education (−)	−.033	−.047	−.009	−.035	+.006	−.027	+.005	−.008
Health (+) Public works (−)	−.053*	−.001	−.021	−.064*	−.022	−.039	+.063*	−.061
Health (+) Foreign relations (−)	−.054*	−.071*	−.038*	−.068*	−.026	−.045	+.023	−.042
Public works (+) Military (−)	+.065*	−.063	−.025	−.006	+.069	+.087	−.033	+.074
Public works (+) Foreign relations (−)	+.019	+.003	−.017	−.038	−.011	−.028	−.032	+.009
Foreign Relations (+) Military (−)	+.047	−.037	.000	+.040	+.091*	+.062	+.006	+.079*

*The numerical entry in each column represents the *b* associated with each loss dummy when all other dummies are included in the equation. The asterisks denote entries with associated probability levels of less than .10.

Conclusion

We sought to determine whether executives' survival needs affected public-sector allocations. The results suggest that in Latin America there exists a kind of "political expenditure cycle." Executives faced with scarce resources respond to sociopolitical conditions and to their own ideological limits by allocating budget shares so as to maximize support when they are most insecure. Political crises are so frequent, however, that there may be little else they can do except struggle to maintain office. The next task in this research is to link survival strategies to ideological preferences and constituency demands, that is, to shift from intraregime cycles to interregime differences.

Notes

1. The expanded version posits a sixth strategy based on conditions encouraging stable shares with a rising total. Its conceptualization is somewhat ambiguous and the results were all quite negative, so I have dropped it from this version. The estimates actually come from the six-strategy model, but they would be only marginally affected if this strategy were dropped.

2. The theoretical basis of this coalition strategy is detailed in the expanded study.

3. A complete listing of the coding of each regime along with relevant monographic citations is found in the expanded study.

4. Typically these data come from the reports of the controllers general of Latin American governments. I have used similar data in "The Politics of Public Spending in Latin America," *American Journal of Political Science,* 21, no. 1, February 1977.

5. The expenditure shares were logged before rates of change and differences were calculated.

Part III
Tax Reform

7 The Normative Bases of Tax Reform: A Constitutional Perspective

Michael L. Goetz

Introduction

Tax reform is necessarily a normative exercise. Equity criteria are explicitly normative while efficiency criteria are implicitly so. This chapter examines the normative bases of tax reform embodied in (1) the quest for a comprehensive tax base,[1] (2) the perfect markets or utilitarian approach,[2] and (3) the fiscal-exchange taxation paradigm.[3] It argues that the apparently disparate views of tax reform in these three views of taxation are explicable when one adopts a constitutional perspective. By viewing tax reform as a mechanism by which constitutionally selected rules can be modified in response to changing circumstances, the properties of tax reform as a means for resolving the inevitable tension between continuity and change can be examined. A constitutional perspective offers the added advantage of unifying positive and normative elements in the analysis of a tax system.[4]

Three Views of Tax Reform

The three views of tax reform to be discussed can be usefully classified in terms of their relative emphasis on equity or efficiency. Proponents of a comprehensive tax base contend that both efficiency and equity would be enhanced if tax reform was structured to eliminate preferential tax provisions. Horizontal equity would be fostered since equal taxes would be paid by taxpayers with equal income regardless of the source of income. That is, those equally situated would be treated equally. Pursuit of a comprehensive tax base would also result in a more efficient tax system, since distortions in resource allocation induced solely by tax advantage would be eliminated. The presumption is that, with a comprehensive tax base, tax rates would be lower, the tax code would be simpler, and thus not only would the tax system be more understandable but administrative and compliance costs would be reduced. The support for "loophole closing" or a comprehensive tax base is surprisingly broad, ranging from the work done at the Brookings Institution to former Secretary of the Treasury William Simon.

The utilitarian or perfect markets approach to taxation stems from the premise that utility provides the only unambiguous measure of welfare. Thus, the utilitarian approach eschews any inferences concerning efficiency or equity based on a listing of desiderata for a tax system. Feldstein demonstrated that an existing tax system will be horizontally equitable if taxpayers can freely adjust their consumption and production activities to the rate structure.[5] The net after-tax reward to apparently differentially treated activities will be identical in utility terms. Therefore, attempts to correct for such apparent horizontal inequities will themselves be horizontally inequitable. Further, when combined with the Pareto criterion for a change in welfare, a substantial degree of rigidity is imparted to a tax system. That is, capitalization eliminates any differential rewards and, accordingly, no gains from trade exist which could form the basis for tax reform. Before complete adjustment has occurred, however, potentially remediable horizontal inequities, and thus tax reform, exist.

In the fiscal-exchange taxation paradigm, the only valid principles of taxation are those derived from the process of individual choice; externally imposed standards of equity or efficiency are spurious. This approach, which derives from Wicksell and Pareto, emphasizes the two-sidedness of the fiscal decision; that is, taxes should be related to expenditures, and be voluntary in nature. Tax reform, intended to modify the tax system to achieve equity or efficiency goals, is a non sequitur; taxes are "reformed" in the fiscal-exchange paradigm by the process of political bargaining among taxpayers. It is possible to interpret the voluntary choice foundations of the fiscal-exchange paradigm in both a current and a more protracted constitutional sense. While we will employ this latter interpretation to unify the three views of tax reform, we will argue that Buchanan's distinction between external standards and voluntarily derived rules is questionable.

The Tax System as Constitutional Choice

Choice at the constitutional level concerns the definition and selection of the rules of the game, as distinct from decisions made within an existing set of rules.[6] It is usually assumed that the rules so selected will remain in force for an extended period of time. Two crucial implications concerning constitutional choice necessarily follow from the presumed quasi-permanent status of such institutions. First, constitutional choice, if not made behind a Rawlsian veil of ignorance, should still be relatively independent of the economic circumstances of the choosers, since over the duration of the rules the economic position of the choosers may change in unpredictable ways. Second, the fact that constitutional choice is necessary at all implies that the costs of making choices in the absence of a constitutional framework would be prohibitive. Presumably, the rules embodied in a constitutional should be permanent in order to foster continuity and stable expectations yet also possess a mechanism by which adjustment to changing circumstances is possible.[7] To resolve this trade-off is the essence of constitutional design.

We contend that the tax system can reasonably be viewed as choice at the constitutional level. The overall structure of the tax system has been relatively unaltered for some time, despite the yearly modifications and tinkering by Congress. Further, resource allocation decisions made as a consequence of a given tax structure are both logically and practically distinct from the choice of the rules of the game, that is, the tax constitution. We must, however, address a potentially fundamental contradiction inherent in this constitutional perspective. Is it possible to reconcile the constitutional imperative to develop rules through a process of mutual agreement with the observed tendency to describe tax systems by the end-state criteria of efficiency and equity? We will argue that the distinction between such externally imposed ethical criteria and those institutions resulting from the individual choice process is largely a spurious one when it is recognized that constitutional choice is properly viewed as an ongoing process.

Constitutional choice as a once-and-for-all decision is a convenient fiction. Transaction and information costs necessarily imply the selection of a system of rules rather than outcomes. However, there is no reason not to expect self-interest to apply to the selection of these rules as well as to decisions made within the rules.[9] "What makes it [constitutional choice] different from day-to-day collective choice is that streams of uncertain outcomes are being compared going well into the future. Constitutional choices are like long-term capital investments."[10]

Therefore, anticipations and expectations concerning these uncertain outcomes are important and will tend to be reflected in the value of the constitution, the capital investment. The constitution must inevitably change as old information is revised or as new information becomes available. This process of revision does not, however, imply that the constitution is thereby invalidated as a quasi-permanent standard. Rather, the function of those rules which define the constitution is to facilitate this process of adjustment to unanticipated contingencies. Accordingly, it is possible to evaluate the adjustment process by criteria such as efficiency or equity. These criteria are not, however, externally imposed but rather follow logically from the imperative to organize economic activity in the presence of those costs which initially dictate constitutional choice.

In our framework, the tax constitution is not static but is rather an ongoing process of readjustment to changing circumstances; tax reform is the vehicle through which such readjustment occurs. Our proffered view of constitutional choice is markedly different from that of Buchanan, who argues that once in place, the constitution may be changed only by mutual consent of the involved parties.[11] We contend that constitutional choice must be necessarily incomplete given less-than-perfect information. This dilemma cannot be resolved by an appeal to rules for choosing since self-interest will necessarily influence the selection of such rules. Combined with the impact of changing information, the constitution evolves according to its own dynamic. We can evaluate tax reform as a means of resolving the inevitable tension between continuity and change employing Hochman's notion of transitional equity;[12] that is, how can change be effected while preserving the expectations of those harmed by the proposed change in the rules. We thus view tax reform as a continuous process rather than a dichotomous, comparative static exercise. The question is not if tax reform occurs but rather who gains and who loses from the continuous process of tax reform.

A Unified Explanation of Tax Reform

We contend that the apparently disparate views on tax reform presented above are explicable when our constitutional perspective is employed. Further, the normative content of the three approaches to tax reform is highlighted by our constitutional framework.

Tax reform for proponents of a comprehensive tax base is synonymous with closing tax loopholes. From a constitutional perspective, loophole closing is not automatically desirable, since such loopholes serve the function of allowing the tax system to adjust to changing economic circumstances. The concept of transitional equity, namely, the preservation of entitlements to preexisting rules while providing a procedure by which the rules of the game may be fairly modified, summarizes the dilemma faced by policymakers. This dilemma is exaggerated by market adjustments in the prices of tax-preferred commodities and the incorporation of such adjustments in the tax constitution. That is, preferential tax treatment will tend to be capitalized, with the result that the apparent gain no longer exists. "Reform" would then reimpose inequities with which the market had come to terms. Adherence to the Pareto rule would, in this case, introduce a degree of rigidity into tax policy. Any proposed tax change is necessarily normative since gains and losses to different groups must be reconciled. Further, to the extent that capitalization is partial rather than complete, the point at which we examine a proposed tax change becomes important. Tax reform is occurring continuously; it cannot be limited to tax reform due to legislative change.

The utilitarian conception of tax reform does recognize the process by which markets can adjust to preferential tax provisions and therefore suggests caution in condemning tax loopholes. However, if the loophole closers ignore market adjustments due to preferential tax provisions, utilitarians ignore the possibility of the anticipation of tax reform on the tax constitution. That is, to the extent that tax reform is anticipated, the tax provision will be "reformed" by the expectation of such reform. Taken together, the loophole-closing and utilitarian notions of tax reform are both simplifications in that they attempt to partition tax reform into before and after reform. Tax reform is, in fact, continuous and moreover serves to foster transitional equity. The normative assumptions of these two approaches are now clear. The loop-hole closing approach gives no primacy to the existing situation while the utilitarian approach attaches absolute primacy to the status quo. A constitutional perspective emphasizes the absence of a unique reference position against which change may be measured.[13] In this context, the apparently halting nature of tax reform is not a vice but is instead a virtue. It is by this device that the tension between stable expectations and the necessity for change, the problem of transitional equity, is resolved. Moreover, such adjustment has both an efficiency and an equity rationale when viewed from a constitutional perspective.

While tax reform is a meaningless construction in the fiscal-exchange paradigm, we can analyze those results as a special case of our interpretation of constitutional choice. Viewing constitutional choice as a once-and-for-all decision, subsequent decisions are constrained by those rules established at the formation of the constitution, and consensus is a reasonable criterion for any subsequent change. However, in a more realistic setting of ongoing constitutional choice dictated by informational inadequacies and transactions costs, self-interest applies to the selection of rules. Self-interest is, in this case, an infinite regress; self-interest applied to the rules to determine the rules, and so on. Our approach does not imply an abandonment of law or an endorsement of either legal positivism or legal normativism.[14] Rather, we have argued that tax reform is a continuous process whose rules we seek to explain. There will invariably be gainers and losers from tax reform. The goal of policy is to balance the gains in rules restructured so as to more effectively reflect current societal decisions against the losses in frustrated expectations and lowered confidence in the rule of law. The process of constitutional adjustment possesses an internal logic; it is not externally mandated. Policy choice in the area of tax reform can be unified with a coherent theoretical model if the constitutional perspective is adopted.

Notes

1. For example, see Stanley S. Surrey, *Pathways to Tax Reform* (Cambridge: Harvard University Press, 1973), and Joseph A. Pechman,

ed., *Comprehensive Income Taxation* (Washington, D.C.: Brookings Institution, 1977).

2. See Martin S. Feldstein, "On the Theory of Tax Reform," *Journal of Public Economics* 6 (July/August 1976): 77–104, and Joseph E. Stiglitz and Michael J. Boskin, "Some Lessons from the New Public Finance," *American Economic Review* 67 (February 1977): 295–301.

3. See James M. Buchanan, "Public Finance and Public Choice," *National Tax Journal* 28 (December 1975): 383–394, and idem, "Taxation in Fiscal Exchange," *Journal of Public Economics* 6 (July/August 1976): 17–29.

4. This unification is especially apparent in the leviathan models of Brennan and Buchanan. See Geoffrey Brennan and James M. Buchanan, "Toward a Tax Constitution for Leviathan," *Journal of Public Economics* 8 (December 1977): 255–273, and idem, "The Logic of Tax Limits: Alternative Constitutional Constraints and the Power to Tax," *National Tax Journal* 32 (June 1979, Supplement): 11–22.

5. This result assumes identical tastes and a single source of income.

6. See James M. Buchanan, *Freedom in Constitutional Contract* (College Station, Tex.: Texas A&M University Press, 1977), especially chapters 6, 7, and 16.

7. Victor Goldberg, "Commons, Clark, and the Emerging Post-Coasian Law and Economics," *Journal of Economic Issues* 10 (December 1976): 877–892.

8. For a discussion of this theme, see P.T. Bauer and A.A. Walters, "The State of Economics," *Journal of Law and Economics* 18 (April 1975): 1–23.

9. See Victor Goldberg, "Institutional Change and the Quasi-invisible Hand," *Journal of Law and Economics* 17 (October 1974): 461–492.

10. Thomas E. Borcherding, "Comments: Session on Bureaucracy," *National Tax Journal* 32 (June 1979, Supplement): 214.

11. See Buchanan, *Freedom in Constitutional Contract.*

12. This concept is defined in Harold M. Hochman, "Rule Changes and Transitional Equity," in *Redistribution through Public Choice,* ed. Harold M. Hochman and George E. Peterson (New York: Columbia University Press, 1974), pp. 320–341.

13. Victor Goldberg, "On Positive Theories of Redistribution," *Journal of Economic Issues* 11 (March 1977): 119–132.

14. Buchanan, *Freedom in Constitutional Contract,* pp. 290–291.

8

Capital-Gains Taxes and Realizations: Can a Tax Cut Pay for Itself?

Gerald E. Auten

Under the U.S. federal income tax, long-term capital gains are taxed at preferential rates and are taxed only when realized rather than as they accrue. These tax provisions have significant effects on investor choices and incentives. Profit-maximizing investors switch investments when prospective investments have a higher expected yield or a preferable risk-return combination than current holdings. If the investor must pay capital-gains taxes on realized gains, this tax wedge may deter some investment switches that could otherwise be profitable. This causes a lock-in effect which tends to slow the turnover of investor portfolios and reduce the realization of accrued gains.

The magnitude of these capital-gains-tax effects has long been an important and controversial question. Most recently, lock-in became an issue during congressional debate on the Revenue Act of 1978 when discussion of the "Laffer curve" suggested that capital-gains-tax rates could be reduced with little or no reduction in tax revenues.

This chapter summarizes previous empirical studies and presents some exploratory new research on the impact of capital-gains taxes on the realization of capital gains.

Previous Empirical Studies

Opinion Studies. Several opinion studies are frequently cited as evidence on investor behavior, but their results are mixed. In a 1953 Harvard Business School study, a minority of all investors, but a majority of high-income investors, indicated that income and capital-gains taxes affected their investment decisions.[1] One-fourth said capital-gains taxes influenced the timing of transactions. A University of Michigan Survey Research Center study of high-income families found that only one-fifth of those with appreciated assets were deterred from selling them by tax considerations.[2]

The research for this study was primarily undertaken while I was a Brookings Economic Policy Fellow in the Office of Tax Analysis, U.S. Treasury Department. I am grateful to Charles Clotfelter, Ralph Bristol, Larry Dildine, Ben Okner, Gene Steuerly, and Janet Auten for comments and assistance.

Polls conducted for the New York Stock Exchange (1960, 1965, 1978) found, however, that investors would be highly responsive to reduced capital-gains taxes. The 1960 survey results implied that a 20-percent cut in capital-gains-tax rates would approximately double Treasury revenues from capital gains and that a 50-percent reduction would produce further revenue increases. During the period of the hearings on the Revenue Act of 1978, Senator Russell Long surveyed thirty-five former high government officials and economic experts, including eight former secretaries of the Treasury.[3] Of the thirty that responded, eighteen indicated that they believed that reducing the percentage of long-term capital gains included in taxable income from 50 to 30 percent would actually increase federal revenues.

Short-Term/Long-Term Differential Studies. Two studies examined taxpayer behavior with regard to the six-month holding period required for taxation at the lower rates that apply to long-term gains. Hinrichs (1963) found that short-term gains as a percentage of total realized security gains are inversely related to the differential between the tax rates that apply to short-term and long-term gains, and concluded that investors were sensitive to tax-rate differences. Fredland, Gray, and Sunley (1968) examined the distribution by number of months held of capital gains realized within one year. They found evidence that investors postpone realization of gains beyond the six-month holding period required to qualify for the lower rates on long-term gains, and found that this effect is stronger in the higher-income brackets. They concluded that there is a six-month lock-in effect that affects the timing of realizations.

Econometric Studies. Feldstein and Yitzhaki (1978) examined the effects of the capital-gains tax on the selling and switching of common stock, using the 1963 Federal Reserve Board Survey of Financial Characteristics of Consumers. They concluded that taxes have a substantial impact on both the decision to sell and the ratio of sales to portfolio size among those who sell. The tax-rate coefficient in the primary equation implied that in the absence of a capital-gains tax, the value of stock sales would approximately triple.

In a second study, Feldstein, Slemrod, and Yitzhaki (1978) used a sample of tax returns to examine the impact of capital-gains taxes on sales and realized gains on corporate stock in 1973. Capital-gains taxes were found to have a very powerful effect on sales of stock, realized stock gains, and the decision to sell among taxpayers with over $3,000 in dividend income. Limiting the long-term tax rate to 25 percent (approximately the pre-1970 capital-gains tax law) was predicted to lead to a near doubling of stock sales and a threefold increase in realized net gains. Tax revenues from capital gains would increase approximately 175 percent. In contrast, taxing long-term gains as ordinary income was predicted to decrease revenues from taxes on stock gains by one-third.[4]

Minarik (1979) used the same data as Feldstein, Slemrod, and Yitzhaki, but found tax effects on corporate stock gains to be much smaller and significant only for taxpayers with at least $20,000 in dividends. The primary differences in Minarik's study were the inclusion of a number of additional independent variables to the estimating equations and a slightly different method of calculating the marginal tax rates on capital gains.

A recent study by Auten and Clotfelter (1979) used a seven-year panel of federal tax returns to examine the transitory and permanent effects of capital-gains taxes on realizations of gains from all sources. This study had three major findings: (1) capital-gains realizations appear to be affected by both transitory and permanent tax-rate effects, (2) the estimated responsiveness for total capital gains is considerably smaller than that found by Feldstein for corporate stock alone, and (3) tax effects on capital losses appear to be qualitatively different than those on capital gains.

A Time-Series Analysis of Capital-Gains Realizations

The basic approach of this study is similar to those used in previous cross-section studies. Realizations of capital gains are specified as a function of the marginal-tax rate on capital gains and other variables that are hypothesized to affect realizations.

The capital-gains realizations and other tax data are drawn from the extensive annual data published by the Internal Revenue Service. This study uses a pooled time series of cross sections by adjusted gross-income class for the years 1952 through 1976. The sample includes taxable returns in five high-income groups with adjusted gross income over $50,000.[5]

Capital-gains realizations are measured as the ratio of gains to adjusted gross income in each income class in each year. Separate equations are estimated for net capital gains and long-term capital gains.

The tax variable used to measure the "price" of realizing gains is the marginal-tax rate applicable to long-term capital gains. It is measured by using the marginal-tax rate for a joint tax return with the average taxable income in that income class in that year.[6] The tax rate on long-term capital gains is one-half the rate on ordinary income or the alternative tax rate, whichever is smaller. This rate is adjusted for tax surcharges in 1952–1953 and 1968–1970. Beginning in 1970, it is also adjusted for the minimum tax and the limitation of the alternative tax to the first $50,000 of long-term gains.

A significant limitation of previous studies of capital gains is that they have used income and wealth variables to measure the ability of taxpayers to realize gains rather than measures of the stock of unrealized gains.[7] This study uses a stock of unrealized gains variable which is based on allocating estimates of the total stock of unrealized gains for households among the various income classes.[8] The stock of unrealized gains is obtained by subtracting realized capital gains from total accrued gains. The total stock of unrealized gains was allocated among the income classes on the basis of dividend income. While dividends are not the only indicator of assets producing capital-gains income, for income classes over \$100,000 most realized gains are from corporate stock.

Additional variables used to explain capital-gains realizations are adjusted gross income net of capital gains and the percentage of the population over age 65. The income variable is included to allow for varying propensities to realize gains by income level. Those over age 65 are more likely to realize gains for consumption purposes and as portfolios are adjusted to yield more current income. On the other hand, the step-up in basis at death on assets bequeathed to heirs provides an incentive not to realize gains.

Results of this study are summarized in table 8–1.[9] The regression coefficients indicate that realizations of capital gains are positively related to the stock of unrealized gains and to the percentage of the population over age 65. They are negatively related to income net of capital gains and to the tax rate on capital gains. The positive sign on the over 65 variable is consistent with the idea that people in this age group are realizing gains for consumption purposes or to readjust their portfolios. The negative sign on income net of gains suggests that people may realize gains in years when other income is lower.

The regression coefficients on the marginal-tax rate in equations 1 and 2 are negative and highly significant. Evaluated at the mean values the elasticities of realization of gains with respect to changes in the tax rate are $-.64$ and $-.66$ for net capital gains and long-term gains, respectively. This implies that a reduction in tax rates would lead to a less than proportionate increase in realized gains.

Equations 1 and 2, however, do not take into account dynamic aspects of capital-gains realizations. If tax rates are known to be higher in the following year, taxpayers may accelerate their plans for realizing gains. Similarly, a temporarily high-tax rate such as a temporary surcharge may induce taxpayers to delay realizations. For tax-policy purposes, it is useful to distinguish between these transitory responses and responses to changes in the permanent tax rate.

To test for transitory as opposed to permanent tax effects, an alternative specification including transitory and permanent tax rates was tested. The permanent tax rate was defined as a three-year-average marginal-tax rate centered on the current year. The transitory tax rate is defined as the difference between the current year tax rate and the permanent tax rate.

Table 8-1
Equations Explaining Capital Gains Realizations, Taxable Returns with Income over $50,000

Independent Variables	Dependent Variables							
	Ratio of Gains to AGI				Logarithm of Gains		Income over $200,000 Ratio of Gains to AGI	
	Net Gains	Long Term	Net Gains	Long Term	Net Gains	Long Term	Net Gains	Long Term
Intercept	6.368 (20.210)	7.721 (39.436)	23.501 (21.532)	47.040 (44.352)	5.077 (1.927)	5.547 (1.844)	10.294 (34.190)	33.711 (65.437)
Tax rate	-.671 (.173)	-1.380 (.365)						
Transitory tax rate			-1.023 (.509)	-2.215 (1.026)	-2.230 (.761)	-2.049 (.769)	-1.354 (1.266)	-4.085 (2.434)
Permanent tax rate			-.423 (.326)	-.884 (.682)	-.876 (.181)	-.839 (.191)	-1.633 (.743)	-3.060 (1.420)
Stock of gains	.571 (.125)	1.109 (.255)	.682 (.146)	1.344 (.299)	1.370 (.081)	1.362 (.082)	.283 (.148)	.628 (.292)
Income	-.028 (.007)	-.055 (.014)	-.027 (.008)	-.051 (.016)	-.281 (.133)	-.258 (.135)	-.022 (.008)	-.047 (.016)
Age 65	5.396 (2.298)	11.657 (4.482)	1.880 (2.547)	3.721 (5.187)	.454 (.851)	.446 (.793)	9.449 (5.179)	16.874 (9.906)

Note: Standard errors of coefficients are in parentheses.

The results are presented in equations 3 and 4. The transitory tax-rate effect is larger than the single tax-rate effect in equations 1 and 2, while the permanent tax-rate effect is smaller. Only the transitory tax-rate effect is found to be significant.

Equations 5 through 8 present evidence using alternative specifications and samples. Equations 5 and 6 are a log linear form of the model with the dependent variables being the logarithm of the average capital gains per return in the income classes. In this specification the coefficients represent elasticities. The estimated tax effects in this specification are somewhat larger than in the basic models, and both the transitory and permanent tax-rate effects are significant.

In equations 7 and 8, the sample is limited to the three highest-income groups, those with income over $200,000. It is these groups that are most likely to be sensitive to tax-rate changes and that were most affected by the increases in capital-gains-tax rates in the 1970 through 1976 period. Both the transitory and permanent tax-rate effects are larger for this group than for the full sample, but the transitory tax variable is not significant.[10]

Conclusions

The variation in the estimated tax effects under alternative specifications is large enough to suggest caution in interpreting the results. However, the results in this study do seem to support several conclusions. Realizations of capital gains for high-income taxpayers do appear to be responsive to capital-gains-tax rates. Both permanent and transitory tax-rate effects can be distinguished. The estimated tax effects are significantly smaller than those found in previous studies of stock gains. Furthermore, Feldstein (1970) found that corporate dividend policy is highly responsive to the relative tax treatment of dividends and retained earnings. Capital-gains-tax reductions would therefore tend to cause dividends to be reduced and thus reduce income-tax revenues from this source. Thus the results of this study are not supportive of the idea that a reduction in capital-gains-tax rates would lead to an increase in total tax revenues.

Notes

1. J. Butters, L. Thompson, and L. Bollinger (1953), chapters 2 and 6.
2. R. Barlow, H. Brazer, and J. Morgan (1966).
3. U.S. Senate, Committee on Finance (1978), pp. 1893–2046.

4. The elasticity of realizations to marginal tax rates is in excess of 4.0, a surprisingly large response.

5. The five adjusted gross-income classes are: $50,000–99,999; 100,000–199,999; 200,000–499,999; 500,000–999,999; and $1,000,000 and over.

6. To make the tax rate exogenous, the marginal rate is calculated using average taxable income less actual capital gains plus average capital gains on returns in that income class for the entire sample period.

7. See, for example, the Feldstein studies and the Minarik study.

8. There are several time-series studies of accrued capital gains. Estimates through 1970 and a projection for 1975 can be found in G. Brannon, N. McClung, and H. Copeland. The variable used in this study is derived from the above study and from Eisner (1976).

9. The use of pooled time-series and cross-section data requires special estimation techniques. The method used is a variation of Aitken's generalized least squares estimation for cross-sectionally correlated timewise autoregressive models. See Kmenta (1971), pp. 512–514.

10. Evaluated at mean values the elasticities of realizations with respect to transitory tax rates were $-.98$ and -1.48 for net gains and long-term gains, respectively, for taxpayers with over $200,000 income. The corresponding permanent tax-rate elasticities were -1.18 and -1.11.

References

Auten, G., and Clotfelter, C. "Permanent vs. Transitory Tax Effects and the Realization of Capital Gains." Unpublished paper, August 1979.

Barlow, R.; Brazer, H.; and Morgan, J. *The Economic Behavior of the Affluent.* Washington: Brookings Institution, 1966.

Brannon, G.; McClung, N.; and Copeland, H. "Unrealized Appreciation Passing at Death." Unpublished paper, no date.

Butters, J.; Thompson, L.; and Bollinger, L. *Effects of Taxation: Investment by Individuals.* Cambridge, Mass.: Harvard University Press, 1953.

Eisner, R. "Capital Gains and Income: Real Changes in the Value of Capital in the United States, 1946–1975." Paper presented at the Conference on Income and Wealth, National Bureau of Economic Research, October 1976.

Feldstein, M. "Corporate Taxation and Dividend Behavior." *Review of Economic Studies* 37, no. 1 (1970): 57–71.

Feldstein, M.; Slemrod, J.; and Yitzhaki, S. "The Effects of Taxation on the Selling of Corporate Stock and the Realization of Capital Gains."

NBER Working Paper No. 250. National Bureau of Economic Research. June 1978.

Feldstein, M., and Yitzhaki, S. "The Effects of the Capital Gains Tax on the Selling and Switching of Corporate Stock." *Journal of Public Economics* 9, no. 1 (1978): 17–36.

Fredland, J.; Gray, J.; and Sunley, E. "The Six Month Holding Period for Capital Gains: An Empirical Analysis of Its Effect on the Timing of Gains." *National Tax Journal* 21, no. 2 (1968): 467–478.

Hinrichs, H. "An Empirical Measure of Investors' Responsiveness to Differentials in Capital Gains Tax Rates among Income Groups." *National Tax Journal* 16, no. 3 (1963): 224–229.

Kmenta, J. *Elements of Econometrics.* New York: Macmillan, 1971.

Minarik, J. "The Federal Income Tax and the Realization of Long-Term Capital Gains." Paper presented at a Conference on Economic Effects of Federal Taxes. Brookings Institution, October 1979.

New York Stock Exchange. "Effects of a Reduced Capital Gains Tax on Locked-in Capital." Summary of a 1960 detailed study by Louis Harris and Associates. New York: mimeographed, no date.

———. "The Effects of Reducing the Capital Gains Tax Rate on Locked-in Capital and Federal Revenues." Summary of a 1965 Study of Investor Attitudes by Louis Harris and Associates. New York: mimeographed, no date.

———. *Public Attitudes toward Investing: A Report by the New York Stock Exchange.* New York: New York Stock Exchange, 1978.

U.S. Senate, Committee on Finance. *Hearings before the Committee on Finance on HR 13511, Revenue Act of 1978,* part 6. Washington: USGPO, 1978.

**Part IV
Fiscal and Monetary Policy**

9 Financing the Government Deficit

Robert H. Rasche

Ever since the pioneering work of Christ, it has been fashionable to introduce a stylized government budget constraint into macroeconomic analysis.[1] The "identity" relating the government deficit or surplus to changes in the outstanding stock of interest-bearing government debt has become so integral a part of the conventional wisdom, that it now enjoys a prominent position in undergraduate macroeconomic theory texts.[2] Given this theoretical prominence, it is surprising that very little attention has been given to measurement of the components of the financing identity.

Most discussion of monetary and fiscal policies characterizes the two as independent instruments of stabilization policy. Strictly speaking, this is true only in the case of marginally balanced-budget fiscal operations. For all other fiscal operations, some source of additional financing must be found. In the particular case of fiscal operations that generate a deficit on the margin, it may be particularly difficult for the monetary authorities to follow an independent policy. Attempts to raise additional financing in private domestic capital markets tend to increase interest rates, all other things equal. Given populist pressure against high or rising interest rates, there is a tendency for the monetary authorities to resist such interest rate movements, and de facto monetize a substantial portion of the marginal deficit by increasing the monetary base. An extreme example of this subservience of the monetary authorities is provided by the commitment of the Federal Reserve System (FRS) to peg interest rates on government securities over the period 1942–1951.

In fact, the linkage between government cash deficits and pressure on the domestic monetary authorities need not be so direct. There are other financing alternatives to private domestic capital markets and monetization of the deficit that are available to the Treasury. Some of these, such as borrowing outside the financial markets at zero-interest rates through various forms of float are primarily short-run or seasonal alternatives. Others, such as market and nonmarket borrowing from foreign governments and monetary authorities can have substantial importance in the long run, and are crucial to understanding the course of foreign as well as domestic monetary policies.

The purpose of this study is to reveal the complexity of the financing identity for the unified budget of the U.S. government, and to attempt to organize the various elements into some meaningful categories. Once these relationships have been identified, the impact of U.S. federal government deficits on domestic and foreign monetary policy can be better understood.

Measurement of the Financing Identity

The basic identity and data for the financing and requirement for the unified budget are found in the Monthly Treasury Statement of Receipts and Expenditures, and in the *Federal Reserve Bulletin*.[3] The first relationship is found in a table titled "Means of Financing." This equation indicates that the

Unified budget deficit (+) or surplus (−)

plus   transactions not applied to the current year's deficit or surplus

equals changes in U.S. government and agency securities held by the public (net of securities held as investments by government accounts)

plus   change in accrued interest payable on public debt securities

plus   changes in deposit funds

plus   changes in miscellaneous liability accounts of the Treasury

less   changes in U.S. Treasury operating cash (including balances held at Federal Reserve banks + tax and loan account balances + demand balances held at other depositories)

less   changes in total holdings of Special Drawing Rights (SDRs) net of changes in SDR certificates issued to Federal Reserve banks

less   changes in gold tranche drawing rights

less   changes in other cash and monetary assets

less   changes in miscellaneous asset accounts of the Treasury

The second identity is the factors affecting bank reserves found in the *Federal Reserve Bulletin*. This identity can be solved for the Treasury balances with the FRS and substituted into the means of financing identity.

Finally, a definition is required for the item transactions not applied to current year's deficit or surplus which appears above. This is perhaps the most elusive component of the whole problem; as far as I can discover, the only place where the data are regularly published is in the *Monthly Treasury Statement*. These three identities can be manipulated to identify the nine categories listed in table 9-1, with the components of each category.

Table 9–1

Sources of Financing U.S. Government Deficits

(+) 1. Borrowing from private capital markets
  a. (+) Borrowing from the public
  b. (−) Changes in Federal Reserve holdings of U.S. government securities
  c. (−) Changes in Federal Reserve holdings of agency issues
  d. (−) Changes in U.S. government securities held by foreign official institutions (from table 3.14, *Federal Reserve Bulletin,* lines 4 and 5). Foreign official holdings of agency issues are not published separately.
  e. (−) Changes in U.S. government securities held by foreign official institutions reported by banks (from table 3.14, *Federal Reserve Bulletin,* line 3).

(+) 2. Change in net source base
  a. (+) Change in member bank deposits at Federal Reserve Banks
  b. (+) Change in currency in circulation
  c. (−) Change in member bank borrowings from the Federal Reserve

(−) 3. Change in Federal Reserve float
  a. (−) Change in deferred availability cash items
  b. (+) Change in cash items in process of collection.

(−) 4. Change in U.S. Treasury cash balances
  a. (+) Change in tax and loan account balances
  b. (+) Change in balances at other depositories (demand)

(+) 5. Change in foreign transaction balances
  a. (+) Change in foreign deposits at the Federal Reserve System
  b. (+) Change in U.S. government securities held by foreign official institutions
  c. (+) Change in U.S. government securities held by foreign official institutions reported by banks
  d. (−) Change in the U.S. gold stock
  e. (−) Change in SDR holdings
  f. (−) Change in Gold tranche drawing rights
  g. (−) Change in Loans to IMF (fiscal 1977 only)

(+) 6. Change in interest accruals
  a. (+) Change in accrued interest payable on U.S. government securities
  b. (−) Conversion of interest receipts on government accounts to accrual

7. Change in excess of miscellaneous F.R. liabilities over miscellaneous assets
  a. (+) Change in other deposits at Federal Reserve Banks
  b. (+) Change in other liabilities of Federal Reserve
  c. (+) Change in Federal Reserve capital accounts
  d. (−) Change in other Federal Reserve loans
  e. (−) Change in acceptances held by Federal Reserve banks
  f. (−) Change in bank premises and operating equipment
  g. (−) Change in other Federal Reserve assets

8. Change in miscellaneous Treasury accounts
  a. (+) Change in Treasury cash
  b. (+) Change in Miscellaneous Treasury liability accounts
  c. (−) Change in other cash and monetary assets of the Treasury
  d. (−) Change in Miscellaneous Treasury asset accounts
  e. (−) Seignorage
  f. (−) Increment on gold
  g. (−) Net gain or loss from U.S. currency valuation adjustment
  h. (−) Net gain or loss from IMF loan valuation adjustment
  i. (−) Change in Treasury currency oustanding

9. Change in deposit funds
  a. (+) Allocations of SDRs
  b. (+) Change in other deposit fund balances

Alternative Sources of Financing

The first category in table 9-1 is an approximation to the volume of funds raised by the Treasury in credit markets from private sources. It is the total amount of Treasury and agency debt issued outside the Treasury less the change in debt holdings by the Federal Reserve and foreign official institutions. The latter is not quite accurate, as it excludes change in holdings of agency debt by such institutions. It is also reasonable that since this is an attempt to measure on a net basis, changes in acceptances held by the FRS (which now appear in category 7) should be subtracted from this grouping.

The second, third, and fifth categories are self-explanatory. The fourth, which involves foreign transactions, probably needs some explanation. The item "foreign official holdings of marketable and nonmarketable Treasury securities" is obtained from the *Federal Reserve Bulletin,* table 3.14, lines 4 and 5. Foreign official holdings of Treasury securities reported by banks is obtained from the *Federal Reserve Bulletin,* table 3.14, line 3. The item "gold tranche drawing rights" is a pseudonym for the U.S. Reserve position in the International Monetary Fund (IMF).[4] Finally "loans to IMF" is a new category with calendar 1977.

Some mention needs to be made of the treatment of swap operations in this framework.[5] When the FRS engages in swap operations, two accounts are involved: foreign deposits at the Federal Reserve and other assets of the FRS.[6] For example, when the FRS obtains foreign currencies in a swap operation both foreign deposits at the FRS and other Federal Reserve assets are increased. Thus the foreign transaction accounts are increased and the excess of Federal Reserve liability over asset accounts is decreased by the swap. Foreign deposits at the FRS have not been accumulated in the past, and are not likely to do so in the future. As these deposits build up, foreign central banks exchange them for nonmarketable Treasury issues, thereby reducing the amount of debt which the Treasury must sell to private economic units by essentially the same amount as would have occurred if the Foreign Central Bank had engaged in the support of the dollar by direct purchase of Treasury securities in the open market.

Categories 6 and 7 are also fairly clear. Category 8 warrants some explanation, since a number of the items are not familiar, and the definitions are not easily available. It is easier to understand the rationale for category 8 by constructing a number of subcategories. Data for some of these subcategories are available only on a fiscal year basis from the Treasury publication *Combined Statement.*[7] The figures presented in table 9-2 are for the transition quarter during 1976.

Of the six categories, the first three can be separately identified from published data. Of these, the first two appear self-explanatory. One modification which may be appropriate to the existing groupings might be to

Table 9–2

Components of the Miscellaneous Treasury Accounts

Miscellaneous Treasury accounts	−319
(−) 1. Capital gains (−)/losses (+)	−137
Increment on Gold	—
Plus: Seignorage	−99
Plus: Net gain (−)/loss (+) from U.S. currency value adjusted	−38
Plus: Net gain (−)/loss (+) from IMF loan value adjusted	—
(−) 2. Miscellaneous cash and monetary assets	−402
Δ Other cash and monetary assets	−386
Less Δ Treasury cash	16
(−) 3. Δ Treasury currency outstanding	169
(+) 4. Δ Deferred and payable interest (net)	167
Δ Deferred interest (premium) on public debt	9
Plus Δ Public debt interest due and payable	90
Less Δ Deferred interest (discount) on U.S. Treasury securities	−68
(−) 5. Treasury float	907
Δ Other miscellaneous assets (receivables, interest)	900
Less Δ Other miscellaneous liabilities (checks outstanding, transit accounts)	−7
(−) 6. Miscellaneous Treasury assets	−51

aggregate the capital gains and losses listed here and the entry allocations of SDRs which is presently combined with deposit fund charges. The entry for allocations of SDRs apparently is the capital gain/loss on U.S. holdings of SDRs.[8]

The third category, the change in Treasury currency outstanding, may appear rather peculiar, particularly since it enters with the same sign as miscellaneous monetary assets held by the Treasury. Treasury currency consists primarily of coin, both inside and outside the Treasury. The term originates from the sources and uses of member bank reserves analysis, and it is offset in that identity by Treasury currency in circulation (a component of currency in circulation), Treasury currency held by Federal Reserve banks, and Treasury currency held by the Treasury (Treasury cash). In the financing identity, changes in the latter are netted out against changes in other cash and monetary assets held by the Treasury.

Two examples help to clarify the role of Treasury currency. First, consider the case where coin in the Treasury vaults is introduced into circulation. (Assume that the Treasury buys bubble gum for all its employees with newly circulated pennies.) This is clearly a means of financing a government expenditure, and should appear as a means of financing. In our identity currency in circulation increases as a result of this operation, but that is all, since Treasury cash nets out in the identity, and Treasury currency outstanding is unchanged. As a second example, consider the production of new coins by the mint with storage in the Treasury vaults. In this case, Treasury currency outstanding is increased, though currency in circulation remains unchanged. Ignoring the marginal costs of operating the mint, the deficit is unchanged by this action, so total financing required must remain unchanged. This in fact happens, because while Treasury currency outstanding is increased, the Treasury's inventory of coinage metals (included in other cash and monetary assets) is reduced and the absolute value of seigniorage is increased. The change in the latter two exactly offset the change in Treasury currency outstanding, so total financing of the budget deficit remains unchanged.

The fourth category, which is not available on a regular basis from published sources, includes interest on the public debt which is due and payable, and two terms which arise out of the peculiarities of the book valuations of Treasury securities. The book valuation of all government securities is at par, not at issue price. Hence, the discrepancy between the book value of the debt issue (changes in which are indicated under I above), and the actual revenue raised from a debt sale has to be accounted for somehow. This is handled in the miscellaneous asset and liability accounts. If debt is sold at a discount (as, for example, with a Treasury Bill auction), then the outstanding value of the debt is increased by the par value of the bills on the books of the Treasury, and the discount is entered as a miscellaneous asset account titled "deferred interest (discount) on marketable U.S. Treasury securities." On the other hand, if a note or bond is issued at a premium, then the par value of the issue is added to the value of the outstanding debt, and a miscellaneous liability item titled "deferred interest (premium) on public debt subscriptions, U.S. Treasury" is increased by the amount of the premium. The changes in these categories, particularly the asset item, have been substantial at times in the recent past, and their character is such that their behavior should not be the random kind of behavior that can be expected from the float-type items which comprise the remainder of the entry.

The fifth subcategory is essentially Treasury float. It represents the excess of receivables and transit items over outstanding checks. The final category is titled "miscellaneous Treasury assets." It appears to be a relatively small account, and I have been unable to track its contents down more specifically. In any case, it is not available separately from the float and interest data except on a fiscal year basis during the last several fiscal years.

The final category is that of deposit funds. Deposit funds are defined as "combined receipt and outlay accounts established to account for receipts that are either (a) held in suspense temporarily and later refunded or paid into some other fund of the government upon administrative or legal determination as to the proper disposition thereof, or (b) held by the government as a banker or agent for others and paid out at the direction of the depositor. Such funds are not available for paying salaries, expenses, grants, or other outlays of the government."[9]

Conclusion

Any attempt to implement the theoretical construct on a government budget constraint must recognize that for the U.S. budgeting practices a simple relationship between the deficit and changes in the stock of high-powered money and the publicly held government debt does not exist. Consideration must also be given to financing from official international sources and through various forms of float. These latter categories have been appreciable sources of financing in recent years.

Notes

1. Carl Christ, "A Simple Macroeconomic Model with a Government Budget Restraint," *Journal of Political Economy* (January/February 1968):53–67.

2. See, for example, R. Dornbusch and S. Fischer, *Macroeconomics* (New York: McGraw-Hill, 1978) chapter 14.

3. Other helpful, though not necessarily complete of accurate tables, can be found in the monthly *Treasury Bulletin.* Additional sources of information of a fiscal year basis are the *Annual Report of the Secretary of the Treasury* and the *Combined Statement of Receipts, Expenditures and Balances of the United States Government.* The latter is the most comprehensive, informative, and probably the most accurate.

4. I am indebted to Wilson Schmidt for tracking down the correspondence between the U.S. Treasury terminology and the more familiar IMF terminology.

5. Particularly since there appears to be considerable misunderstanding on the implications of federal support actions for the dollar, for the amount of debt which the Treasury will have to sell. See particularly "Investment Flow in U.S. Money Markets May Alter Drastically as Dollar Gets Aid," *Wall Street Journal,* 11 January 1978.

6. See Federal Reserve Bank of New York, *Glossary: Weekly Federal Reserve Statements,* p. 18.

7. Table A, schedule 1.

8. Again this discovery is the result of Wilson Schmidt's painstaking reconciliation of Treasury and IMF data sources.

9. *Combined Statement of Receipts, Expenditures and Balances of the United States Government,* 1976, p. 3.

10 The Interface of Fiscal and Monetary Policy

Henry C. Wallich

This chapter examines the interface between fiscal and monetary policy, in the context of a book on taxation and spending policy. Fiscal and monetary policy are generally regarded as the two principal macroinstruments available to policymakers in a market economy. It should be noted to begin with, therefore, that the distinction is in important respects institutional rather than economic. Fiscal policy works through the budget deficit or surplus as well as the level of the budget. Monetary policy works through its effects on money supply, credit, and interest rates. However, both affect the level of economic activity principally by affecting aggregate demand. They work in the same dimension, and thus are substitutes for each other. In this broad sense, they represent one instrument rather than two, capable of attaining only one principal goal: the rate of utilization of the economy's capacity. The two policies have side effects that differ significantly, for instance, with respect to economic growth and the balance of payments. It is mainly because of these differing side effects that the two policies can be regarded as separate instruments and employed to attain two separate goals.

Keynesian versus Monetarist Views

Since fiscal and monetary policy are in a major respect substitutes, the question of their relative effectiveness needs to be addressed. Views on the strength of the two instruments have changed dramatically during the postwar years. To some extent, wide differences of views persist today. The popular distinction between monetarists on one side and Keynesians (or fiscalists) on the other captures the essence of this difference of views. In the early postwar years as well as during the late 1930s, few economists would have disagreed with the proposition that fiscal policy was far and away the senior and more powerful member of the team. The "rediscovery of money" came gradually, at least in Anglo-Saxon and Scandinavian countries. As interest rates rose, idle balances became more costly and the demand for money thus became more susceptible to monetary policy. This shifted the empirical base of much of the debate in favor of the monetarists and against the Keynesians. Accelerating inflation since the middle 1960s has helped to make many of the monetarists' propositions widely persuasive.

Upon closer inspection, much of the difference in views between the two camps turns on the measurement of monetary policy.[1] The Keynesian view of monetary policy has traditionally focused on control of interest rates. The monetarist approach focuses on the quantity of money. The question whether fiscal or monetary policy is stronger depends decisively on this alternative standard.

In the Keynesian framework, which had dominated American policy thinking at least until the end of the 1960s, a constant monetary policy is a policy that keeps interest rates constant. A fall in interest rates is interpreted as easing, a rise as tightening. It might be noted that this is even today very much the interpretation given to monetary policy by the financial markets and the press.

In the monetarist world, a constant monetary policy means a constant rate of growth of the money supply. Acceleration of money-supply growth means easing, deceleration means tightening, regardless of whether these actions are accompanied by rising or falling or constant interest rates, any of which scenarios is quite possible. The Federal Reserve in 1970 shifted from an approach stressing mainly interest rates to one stressing mainly the money supply, with a proviso that the federal-funds rate not fluctuate in too wide a range.[2] This shift did not seem to alter the market's perception very much. Money supply targets were specified, which the Federal Open Market Committee (FOMC) and, under the FOMC's instructions, the open-market manager implemented by moving the federal funds rate. In October 1979, the Federal Reserve shifted to a very predominant emphasis on the money supply but so far has found it difficult to persuade the market to adopt the money supply rather than interest rates as a yardstick of Federal Reserve policy.

Given these alternative definitions of constant, easy, and tight monetary policies, different conclusions as to the relative strength of fiscal and monetary policy are inevitable. If fiscal policy is expansive while monetary policy, as represented by interest rates, is unchanged, aggregate demand will almost certainly increase. The Keynesian view would take this as evidence that fiscal policy, with monetary policy neutral, can achieve a significant effect. But, of course, with expansive fiscal policy interest rates can be held constant, if at all, only by an injection of money, whether we view this as a means of financing the deficit or simply as an addition to overall liquidity. Given the monetarist definition of monetary policy, this is an expansive monetary policy. If the money supply is not increased, an expansive fiscal policy, through the associated government borrowing and general increase in activity, will raise interest rates. Some private expenditures would then be crowded out. It could not be said with assurance how much, if at all, aggregate demand would increase. Fiscal policy, unsupported by monetary policy, might thus have little power. If both expand simultaneously, one could debate which of the two was the cause of the ensuing expansion. Monetarists would tend to argue that while fiscal expansion accomplishes little or nothing without monetary expansion, the same monetary expansion unaccompanied by fiscal expansion would have much the same effect by expanding private demand. The higher the rate of inflation, and the more probable, therefore, that any increase in the money supply will be spent rather than kept idle, the more plausible becomes the monetarist case.

Burden Sharing

Central bankers can often be heard to blame government deficits for the high rate of inflation. Likewise, it is commonplace for central bankers to assert that they cannot or should not carry the entire burden of fighting inflation. Monetary policy cannot do the job all by itself.[3] A strong fiscal policy, reducing the deficit, is needed. Such views may be founded on either politics or economics. In any event, they tend to place central bankers in the Keynesian camp where fiscal policy is regarded as important. On the other hand, if nothing matters but the money supply, then government borrowing can do no more damage than private borrowing provided the central bank firmly controls the money supply. It is perhaps not surprising, therefore, that there is strong support for monetarist views in the U.S. Congress which implicitly exonerate Congress from responsibility for inflation.

Extreme positions, nevertheless, tend to oversimplify the conclusions. In the abstract, the central bank, adhering firmly to an appropriate money-supply target, should be able to overcome most if not all the expansive effects of a rising budget deficit and government borrowing. It can do this only, however, at the expense of rising interest rates and a progressive crowding out of private expenditures. The crowding out may not occur immediately, if there is sufficient unused capacity in the economy. That was the case in 1975, when predictions of massive crowding out by the mounting federal deficit proved erroneous. But in any event, it is not politically easy for the central bank to conduct a money-supply policy that entails sharply higher interest rates, even if the government deficit is the initiating factor. The chances are that the central bank, in trying to moderate the rise in interest rates, will overshoot its money-supply target. In that sense, then, it will be financing the government deficit whether or not it views itself as financing the government directly. A restrictive fiscal policy reduces the burden upon monetary policy and so may be an essential condition of overcoming inflation. It might be added that in the absence of fiscal restraint, the central bank may have to slow down the rate of growth of the money supply beyond what would otherwise be appropriate in order to raise the crowding-out effect to a level high enough to offset the fiscal expansion.

Growth and the Fiscal-Monetary Mix

Fiscal and monetary policy both work on aggregate demand. But they do so in different ways. As a result, different effects on long-run economic growth can be achieved by "changing the mix," that is, substituting one instrument for the other to a greater or lesser extent, while keeping aggregate demand unchanged. Monetary policy works principally on capital expenditures, that is, those financed with credit or out of savings. It thus affects principally, though not exclusively, investment. Fiscal policy, to the extent that it involves changes in the level of taxation, affects principally consumption, since most, though by no means all, taxes affect real-disposable personal income. A mix of easy money—tight budgets will tend to favor investment and to restrain consumption. A tight money–easy budgets policy favors consumption at the expense of investment.[4]

There is little need to inquire what has been the U.S. mix in recent years. Budgets have been easy, with only two surpluses since 1960. Whether monetary policy has been tight or not may be debatable, but by such qualitative comparison as can be made monetary policy surely has been the tighter of the two. This has contributed to the general proconsumption-antisaving and investment bias of the American economy and presumably to the slowdown in the rate of growth of productivity and potential gross national product (GNP) in recent years.

Fiscal policy by itself can, of course, lean toward more investment or more consumption for any given level of the budget and its deficit or surplus. Both taxes and expenditures can be oriented more in one direction or the other. But changes in the volume of saving and investment that can be induced by changing the incidence or the progressivity of taxes and the content of government expenditures seem to be quite limited in comparison to the total volume of receipts and expenditures. The impact on available saving resulting from a greater or smaller budget deficit can be very large once deficits approach the levels of 20 percent of the budget and 5 percent of GNP as during the middle 1970s. An important condition for shifting resources out of the public sector and into private investment is, of course, that aggregate demand is maintained at an appropriate level.

The possibility of changing the fiscal-monetary mix in favor of investment or consumption does not depend on the adoption of a Keynesian or monetarist point of view. Under both approaches, a larger budget deficit means higher-interest rates which hurt growth, and vice versa. Under both approaches, too, a lower deficit can be turned into more private investment, though under the Keynesian interpretation a more stimulative monetary policy would probably be required to keep aggregate demand unchanged.

The Mix and the Balance of Payments

The antigrowth character of the recent U.S. fiscal-monetary mix has, on the other hand, favored a stronger balance of payments and stronger dollar, compared with balance-of-payments implications of a growth-oriented mix. The tight money—easy budgets mix implies higher-interest rates. These attract capital and improve the balance of payments under both fixed and floating rates. In general, therefore, if the balance of payments is of concern to the policymaker, the classical prescription is that monetary policy should be assigned to influencing the balance of payments and fiscal policy to regulate the level of economic activity. With two instruments, two goals can be achieved.[5]

Of course, if the effects of monetary and fiscal policy on the domestic economy and on the balance of payments can be predicted with exactitude, such a selective assignment of instruments to objectives is not necessary. Both instruments can be set simultaneously in order to achieve the desired objective. But the required information usually, of course, is not available.

The favorable effect on the balance of payments flowing from selective assignment of monetary policy is likely to be short-lived. Capital flows imply lack of balance in the current account. The level of international indebtedness is affected and so may be the stock of capital. Over time, therefore, a policy mix designed to strengthen the balance of payments by attracting foreign capital may require frequent adjustments in interest or exchange rates.

Fiscal and Monetary Policy under Fixed and Floating Rates

For the United States, as a reserve currency country, the effectiveness and the modus operandi of fiscal or monetary policy for achieving a desired level of aggregate demand is not significantly different under alternative regimes of fixed and floating exchange rates. That, however, is not the case for other countries. For those countries fixed rates mean pegging to a particular reserve currency that must be bought and sold without limit in order to maintain exchange-rate parity, while floating means to have no such commitment. Assuming a high degree of international mobility of capital, the effectiveness of fiscal and monetary policy under the two regimes differs strikingly.[6] If a country with fixed exchange rates seeks to tighten monetary policy by slowing the money supply and/or raising interest rates, it attracts a large volume of foreign capital. By converting this inflow into local currency, as it must, it nullifies the initial restrictive effect. The reverse happens if the country tries to ease. Monetary policy, in effect, is paralyzed. If instead the country attempts to contract excess demand by reducing its budget deficit with the money supply unchanged, aggregate demand will decrease, the demand for money and therefore interest rates will fall, and the ensuing outflow of capital will prevent monetary ease and will help fiscal policy to operate with maximum effectiveness. The same principles hold on the stimulative side.

Under floating rates, net international capital movements are not possible except where a current account deficit or surplus exists. Fiscal expansion will raise interest rates, but the ensuing efforts to foreigners to acquire the local currency will simply push up the exchange rate. A current account deficit results which nullifies the expansionary effects of fiscal action. Monetary policy, on the other hand, can now effectively determine the money supply and/or interest rates because no monetization of international flows is required. Any tendency for interest-rate differentials to change, however, will lead to exchange-rate movements and these will lead to current account surpluses or deficits. The restraining or expansive effect of monetary policy then is enhanced by a shift in the trade balance which is induced by the corresponding exchange-rate movements. Monetary policy becomes effective with floating rates.

The conditions of the conceptual framework are not likely to be fully realized, of course. Full international mobility of capital prevails for very few countries. Nor have countries been willing to allow their exchange rates to float cleanly, which has tended to fudge the distinction between fixed and floating rates. The size of a country relative to the world economy also makes a difference: small countries must accept the full adjustment resulting from any change, large countries can shift part of the burden of adjustment to the rest of the world. Most countries maintain some degree of fixity of exchange rate with respect to one or a nucleus of countries while floating with respect to the rest of the world. All this has in practice limited the significance of the foregoing analysis. But numerous examples could be cited for countries other than the United States of periods during which the analysis laid out above accurately described events.

Fiscal and Monetary Policy in Long-Run Equilibrium

In long-run equilibrium, the concept of monetary policy as an interest-rate policy rather than a money-supply policy is hard to sustain. It begs the question what effects the change in money supply that is needed to achieve any particular interest rate may have upon prices and other economic variables.

Price changes produce changes in inflation expectations and nominal inter-est rates and deprive the central bank of its power to peg a particular inter-est rate for a sustained period of time if that rate is inconsistent with infla-tion expectations and the real return on capital.

Any rate of growth of nominal money supply, on the other hand, can be sustained by the monetary authorities indefinitely, assuming a floating exchange rate or unvarying reserve currency status of the country in ques-tion. Money-supply growth determines the rate of inflation, and the rate of inflation determines nominal interest rates. All real variables of the econ-omy, including the rate of GNP growth, become independent of monetary policy in such a long-run equilibrium situation, since monetary policy can-not durably affect the real-interest rate.

In that situation, the role of monetary policy in determining the real-interest rate is taken over by fiscal policy. A large deficit, absorbing capital market funds, makes capital scarce for the private sector and raises the real-interest rate. A budget surplus increases the supply of capital and lowers the real-interest rate. There is then left only one instrument—fiscal policy—which in effect takes over the function exercised by monetary policy in the short run: to determine the real-interest rate.

While the United States no doubt is nowhere near any long-term equil-ibrium, at present high rates of inflation the relation between fiscal and monetary policy is fairly close to that of the long-run equilibrium model. So long as the Federal Reserve pursues a policy that sustains existing inflation expectations, it has very little influence even over nominal interest rates. Its influence over short-term rates is somewhat greater than over long-term rates. But broadly speaking, its only means of significantly influencing interest rates under conditions of high inflation is to pursue a policy that changes inflation expectations. Monetary policy, under these conditions, in any sense other than determination of the rate of inflation, is made mainly by fiscal policy. At the present time, this policy in the United States is a low-growth policy. So long as the federal government borrows around 2 percent of GNP, in an economy whose net savings amount to about 5 percent of GNP, and spends it for mainly consumptive purposes, capital will be scarce for the private sector and real-interest rates will be higher than they would be under a policy of budget balance or even more one of debt repayment.

Notes

1. See Sherman J. Maisel, *Managing the Dollar* (New York: W.W. Norton and Co., 1973), especially chapters 3, 10–12, and Karl Brun-ner, ed., *Targets and Indicators of Monetary Policy* (San Francisco: Chandler Publishing Co., 1969).

2. For a history of Federal Reserve operating procedures see Henry C. Wallich and Peter M. Keir, "Operating Guides in U.S. Monetary Policy: A Historical Review," *Federal Reserve Bulletin* 65 (September 1979): 679–691.

3. For one policymaker's view of this topic, see Arthur F. Burns, "The Anguish of Central Banking," the 1979 Per Jacobsson Lecture in Belgrade, Yugoslavia (Washington: Per Jacobsson Foundation—IMF, 30 September 1979).

4. On these issues see Martin Feldstein, "Tax Rules and Mismanagement of Monetary Policy," NBER Working Paper No. 422 (Cambridge: NBER, 1979).

5. For example, see R.A. Mundell, "Appropriate Use of Monetary and Fiscal Policy for Internal and External Stability," *IMB Staff Papers* 9 (1962), no. 1.

6. R.A. Mundell, *International Economics* (New York: Macmillan, 1968), pp. 250–271.

**Part V
The Politics of Taxing
and Spending**

11 Partisanship and Ideology in the Revenue Act of 1978

Henry C. Kenski

Introduction

The Revenue Act of 1978 underscores the fact that cutting taxes is a compli-
cated business and that Congress can reject administration initiatives in
favor of its own alternatives. The year 1978 was frequently called the year
of the taxpayers' revolt, with statewide tax-cutting propositions in California and elsewhere, and political candidates promising large tax cuts elsewhere across the country. Curiously, the tax-cut bill passed by Congress
reflected the atmosphere in appearance only. As Cohen and Havemann
observe, "Although it includes a record of $18.7 billion in 1979 tax reduc-
tions, the bill will not even offset the combined impact of inflation and
social security tax increases for most taxpayers."[1] The year began with
President Carter introducing the most innovative and controversial part of
his economic package, the centerpiece calling for tax cuts of $33.9 billion
and revenue-raising recommendations of $9.4 billion. Hoping for increased
economic growth without higher inflation, a more progressive tax system,
and enough overall relief to discourage a middle-class backlash, Carter's
proposed $24.5 billion net tax reduction was designed to walk a political
and economic tightrope.[2] His package encountered obstacles almost
immediately and he was forced to abandon many of his proposed
"reforms" (revenue-raisers). The ensuing battle matched the White House
against Capitol Hill and involved differences over the size of the tax reduction as well as who the major beneficiaries should be. Party partisanship
and ideology both played a role in the final outcome. The purpose here is to
explain the different roles played by the president, House, and Senate in the
Revenue Act of 1978.

The President

Like his Democratic predecessors, Kennedy and Johnson, President Carter
believed that the federal government's fiscal powers (taxing and spending)
could and should be used to affect changes in the country's economy. His
view of tax policy was a broad one, and encompassed considerations of
economic growth as well as revenue. Carter's concern with tax reform dated

to the 1976 presidential campaign, when he called for a tightening of what
he deemed loopholes, and used such pejorative symbols as the "three-mar-
tini lunch" to denounce existing inequities. In outlining his 1978 tax package, he argued that "fundamental reform of our tax laws is essential and
should begin now," but also stressed economic growth by suggesting that
"the enactment of these proposals will constitute a major step toward sus-
taining our economic recovery and making our tax system fairer and
simpler."[3] In short, Carter hoped by his proposals to improve equity and to
promote economic growth without exacerbating inflation by a $24.5 billion
net tax cut and certain revenue-raising reforms.

The Carter package encountered resistance from Congress because
many members "were troubled that so large a tax reduction would contribute to an unacceptable increase in the budget deficit and would also spur the
already high rate of inflation."[4] Moreover, Congress was continually
pressed for middle-class tax-relief measures, such as a rollback of the
scheduled social-security tax increases, reduction in capital-gains taxes, and
a proposed educational-expense tax credit, all of which Carter opposed.[5]
Since 1978 was a midterm election year and middle- and upper-class voters
were more likely to vote than lower-income citizens,[6] there was good reason
for Congress to be unenthusiastic about Carter's reform proposals. Even
strong advocates of tax reform, such as House Democrat Abner Mikva,
conceded that the political climate was not right for reform and that
"there's just not a constituency for it."[7] Consequently, Congress dropped
many of Carter's revenue-raising reform proposals and by May, Carter had
agreed to scale back the proposed cut ot $19.4 billion.

The Congress

In July, the House Ways and Means Committee met to consider the Carter
package and an alternative proposal, known as the Jones compromise,
introduced by Chairman Al Ullman, ranking Republican Barber Conable,
and Oklahoma Democrat James P. Jones. The latter was endorsed by the
Ways and Means Committee after minor modifications. It called for net tax
cuts for individuals and businesses of $15.4 billion in 1979 and succeeded
from considerable coalition-building, as the committee's twelve Republicans joined thirteen Democrats on a 25–12 vote. *Congressional Quarterly* noted that "the bill bore almost no resemblance to the tax program
Carter sent to Congress in January. It excluded almost all of the president's
proposed tax reforms, aimed the benefits of the tax cut primarily toward
people in the middle- and upper-income brackets rather than lower down
the income scale as suggested by Carter, and included capital-gains-tax
reductions that the president threatened to veto."[8]

With the Democrats divided, Republicans strove to win support in the House and Senate for their own Kemp-Roth proposal for a very large reduction in individual and corporate income-tax rates averaging 30 percent to be phased in over three years. This proposal was not accompanied by spending reductions, and instead relied on optimistic assumptions of the cut's effect on savings, investment, labor supply, and increased productivity. Like the new economics of Kennedy and Johnson, Kemp-Roth was designed to increase national output, national income, and therefore the tax yield to the federal government. Unlike the former, it was put forth in a period of high inflation, and it enabled Democratic politicians and an overwhelming majority of economists to declare it highly inflationary and unable to generate the tax revenues expected by its supporters.[9]

With their party divided, liberal House Democrats rallied behind the so-called Corman amendment to provide an $18.1 billion tax cut, including increased benefits to taxpayers earning less than $50,000, and particularly to those earning less than $15,000. Minnesota Republican Bill Frenzel called it the major tax bill showdown and said, "The Corman amendment redistributes income. The Committee bill cuts taxed evenly,"[10] In the end, the House approved a $16.3 billion tax cut that was basically the "Jones Compromise," sharply dividing Democrats but winning general Republican support. The final floor vote was 362–49, with Republicans labeling the administration "irrelevant" to the outcome, and most Democrats keeping their distance from the president. Kemp-Roth was defeated by a vote along party lines, 177–240, while the Corman amendment lost by a closer margin of 193–225. House Speaker O'Neill made a rare floor speech supporting the latter bill and faulted the administration for its tardy performance.[11] Ohio Democrat Charles Vanik was harsher yet, claiming that "the President and his advisors were totally naive about the legislative process."[12]

As Robert Samuelson observes, "The Senate and House regularly go through a ritual in which the House enacts lower tax cuts—allowing House Members to advertise their 'fiscal responsibility'—and the Senate enlarges the total, allowing everyone to take credit for being generous,"[13] This scenario was faithfully followed in 1978 as the Senate boosted the cuts to $29.1 billion before sending it to be scaled back in the House-Senate conference committee. The Republican-inspired Kemp-Roth-proposal was rejected 36–60, but the Bumpers amendment to cut individual income taxes $4.5 billion more than the $16 billion recommended by the Senate Finance Committee was approved 52–43. Its objective was similar to the Corman amendment in the House, as it sought relief for persons with incomes below $50,000, especially those in the $16,000 to $36,000 range.[14] The House and Senate conferees bargained to an $18.7 billion tax cut agreement that came much closer to the House-passed $16.3 billion package.[15] The final product was clearly a tax policy written by Congress, not the president, and was based on a broad coalition of moderate and conservative Democrats uniting with Republicans. This bipartisanship was precipitated by ideological differences within the Democratic Party (largely northern liberals versus southern conservatives) and between the president and Congress over the tax cut's size and primary beneficiaries.

Partisanship and Ideology

Our final concern is to examine the relative importance of party and ideology via roll-call analysis of the major floor amendments to the 1978 Revenue Act. Political divisions over tax-cut size are reflected in the Kemp-Roth proposal, while differences over the preferred beneficiaries are captured by the Corman amendment in the House and Bumpers amendment in the Senate. Partisanship is measured by party affiliation, while the measure for ideology draws upon the conservative coalition support and conservative coalition opposition scores for each member published by *Congressional Quarterly*. These scores are based on a large number of annual roll calls encompassing various domestic and foreign policy domains; the two-year averages for the 95th Congress involved 156 roll calls in 1977 and 164 in 1978.[16] Both conservative coalition support and opposition scores penalize for absences, but as both are compiled they can be used in tandem to remove the effect of absence on scores. The computational variation employed "is produced by dividing the support score of a member by the sum of his support and opposition scores."[17] The results comprise conservative coalition support ratios used to classify members as liberals (0–30), moderates (31–70), and conservatives (71–100). Moderates and conservatives are also combined into a nonliberal category for purposes of tabular analysis.

The data in table 11–1 suggest that ideological divisions in Congress are such that building a majority coalition for liberally oriented tax-cut and tax-reform legislation is not easy. They further indicate that the Senate is slightly more liberal than the House, that northern Democrats are considerably more liberal than their southern counterparts in both chambers, that southern Democrats are slightly less conservative than Republicans in the House but somewhat more conservative than the GOP in the Senate, and that Republicans are slightly less conservative in the Senate than in the House. Overall, the dominant orientation of Republicans and Southern Democrats is decisively conservative, while northern democrats constitute a bulwark of liberalism.

Table 11–2 demonstrates that party and ideology were both significant in the Kemp-Roth vote in each chamber, though partisanship was slightly more important. The vote on tax-cut benefits shows that party and ideology

Table 11–1
Ideological Divisions in the 95th Congress, 1977–1978 (in percentages)

	All Members	Northern Democrats	Southern Democrats	All Democrats	Republicans
House					
Liberals	34	69	9	50	2
Moderates	27	29	33	30	20
Conservatives	39	2	58	20	78
N	(434)	(197)	(90)	(287)	(147)
Senate					
Liberals	36	75	0	52	11
Moderates	24	23	32	26	21
Conservatives	40	2	68	22	68
N	(100)	(43)	(19)	(62)	(38)

Table 11–2
Partisanship and Ideology in the 95th Congress: Percentage Tax-Cut Support (Kemp–Roth) and Tax-Cut Benefits (Corman in the House and Bumpers in the Senate)

	Democrats	Republicans	Liberals	Nonliberals
Tax-cut support				
House				
Yes	13.5	97.9	5.0	61.6
No	86.5	2.1	95.0	38.4
N	(274)	(143)	(141)	(276)
Gamma	− .99		− .94	
Senate				
Yes	11.7	80.6	5.9	54.8
No	88.3	19.4	94.1	45.2
N	(60)	(36)	(34)	(62)
Gamma	− .94		− .90	
Tax-cut benefits				
House				
Yes	67.0	5.6	96.5	20.3
No	33.0	94.4	3.5	79.7
N	(276)	(142)	(142)	(276)
Gamma	.94		.98	
Senate				
Yes	66.1	36.1	82.4	39.3
No	33.9	63.9	17.6	60.7
N	(59)	(36)	(34)	(61)
Gamma	.55		.76	

both retained their significance in the House, with a slight edge given to the salience of ideology. In the Senate, however, the relationship between party and tax-cut benefits was unimpressive, while that between ideology and tax-cut benefits was a modest one. Votes on the Republican-sponsored Kemp-Roth bill illustrate that ideological divisions are more pronounced if the two parties take an official position that invokes partisan cues and reinforces the linkage between party and ideology, a condition not present in either the Corman or Bumpers amendment. The data also suggest that the less conservative orientation of Senate Republicans played an important role in weakening the party/tax-cut benefits relationship. Finally, data disaggregation by party for all three ideological groups on the Bumpers amendment reveal that partisanship is not a potent constraint on any of the groups in the Senate, nor on House liberals or conservatives on the Corman amendment. House liberals in both parties heavily favored the amendment, while House conservatives in both parties strongly opposed it. Party does have an influence on House moderates, however, as 58 percent of eightyfive Democratic moderates supported Corman compared to only a miniscule 14 percent of twenty-eight Republican moderates.

Conclusion

(1) The Revenue Act of 1978 was basically a tax policy written in Congress and supported by a broad coalition of moderate and conservative Democrats uniting with Republicans. (2) This support was precipitated by ideological differences within the Democratic Party and between the president and Congress over the tax cut's size and primary beneficiaries. (3) Ideological divisions in Congress are such that building a majority coalition for liberally oriented tax-cut and tax-reform legislation is difficult. (4) Party and ideology were both salient in the Kemp-Roth vote in each chamber and also in the Corman vote in the House. In the Senate, the party and tax-cut benefits finding was unimpressive, while a modest relationship emerged between ideology and the latter.

Notes

1. Richard E. Cohen and Joel Havemann, "A Tax 'Cut' Bill That's a Cut in Name Only," *National Journal* 10 (21 October 1978):1678.
2. Robert J. Samuelson, "Carter's Tax Tightrope," *National Journal* 10 (28 January 1978):133.
3. "Congress Challenges Carter Tax Proposals," *Taxes, Jobs, and Inflation* (Washington, D.C.: *Congressional Quarterly,* 1978), p. 21.

4. Ibid.

5. Ibid.

6. For the 1978 turnout see "Renters Inclined to Skip Elections, Survey Finds," *Wall Street Journal,* 18 October 1979, p. 6.

7. "Congress Challenges Carter," p. 24.

8. Ibid., p. 26.

9. Robert W. Hartman, "Kemp-Roth and All That," *Taxing and Spending* 11 (February 1979):12–18.

10. "Taxes: House Hands Carter Another Defeat," *Congressional Quarterly Weekly Report* 36 (12 August 1978):2097.

11. Ibid., p. 2098.

12. Ibid., p. 2095.

13. Robert J. Samuelson, "The Games Congress Plays," *National Journal* 10 (23 September 1978):1520.

14. "Senate Boosts Tax Cut to $29.1 Billion," *Congressional Quarterly Weekly Report* (14 October 1978):2933–2939.

15. Cohen and Havemann, "A Tax 'Cut' Bill," pp. 1678–1679.

16. Data come from various issues of *Congressional Quarterly Weekly Report.* Their thirteen state classification of the South is used.

17. Norman J. Ornstein, Robert L. Peabody, and David W. Rohde, "The Changing Senate: From the 1950s to the 1970s," in *Congress Reconsidered,* ed. Lawrence C. Dodd and Bruce J. Oppenheimer (New York: Praeger Publishers, 1977), p. 19.

12 Assessing Congressional Budget Reform: The Impact on Appropriations

Mark W. Huddleston

In July 1974, the U.S. Congress established a new ` set of budget-making procedures under the aegis of the Congressional Budget Reform and Impoundment Control Act (CBRICA).[1] Supported by a broad coalition of conservatives interested in fiscal restraint and liberals concerned about priorities in federal spending, the legislation passed by overwhelming votes in both houses, and left in its wake high expectations about a resurgent congressional role in federal budgeting. Although this reform has attracted considerable scholarly interest, few systematic attempts have been made to gauge the effects of the legislation on budgetary outcomes.[2] This chapter makes a preliminary effort to do so by assessing changes in patterns of federal appropriations. My principal finding is that, contrary to expectations, the CBRICA has neither enhanced congressional autonomy nor fundamentally restructured House-Senate roles in the appropriations process.

Hypotheses and Data

Although the CBRICA's supporters differed in several important respects over the intent of budget reform, there was general agreement on two points regarding the expected impact of reform on the appropriations process. First, Congress was to be made more independent of the president in setting budget policy; the two Budget Committees and the Congressional Budget Office (CBO) were to provide Congress with the analytical capabilities necessary to permit reduced dependence on the fiscal projections and budget estimates prepared by the Office of Management and Budget (OMB) and the rest of the executive establishment. Second, the CBRICA was to inject a greater degree of "rationality" into the system, and make congressional budgeting less subject to the incrementalist rituals that had characterized it in the past; the spring budget targets, summer "scorekeeping" operations, and fall spending ceilings, together with a streamlined appropriations schedule, were designed at least in part to discipline the expenditure process and force a more systematic consideration of spending trade-offs. If these expectations have been met and the CBRICA has had the intended effects in these two core areas, we would hypothesize that there will have been, since 1974, (1) a decreased correspondence between presidential budget requests and congressional appropriations, and (2) an increased correspondence between the preconference appropriations totals passed by the House and those passed by the Senate.[3] The second hypothesis derives from the assumption that the existence of common budget targets should reduce the propensity of the House to act as a "budget cutter" and the Senate to play the role of "appeals court."[4]

To test these hypotheses, data on presidential requests and congressional action were gathered for each of the eleven major annual appropriations bills for fiscal years 1966–1979.[5] The appropriations bill was selected as the unit of analysis because it provides a measure that is at once accessible and reasonably consistent, virtues that are not combined in data drawn from appropriations accounts or breakdowns of the budget by function. For each of fiscal years 1966–1978, appropriations figures were taken, with minor adjustments, from the annual summaries in the *Congressional Quarterly Almanac;* fiscal 1979 data were gleaned from the 9 October 1978 *Senate Budget Scorekeeping Report* (No. 79-10).[6]

Findings

Congressional Control of the Purse. Contrary to expectations, the CBRICA has not increased congressional autonomy in appropriations decisions. If we compare the differences between the percentage increases over the previous year's total appropriations requested by the president and allowed by Congress (table 12-1), we find in fact that Congress has moved marginally closer to presidential requests since FY 1975; indeed, the mean difference has declined from prereform to postreform periods by more than a full percentage point at each stage of the process.

Nor does this pattern simply represent changes in some appropriations bills canceling out changes in others. As we can see in Table 12-2, for seven of the bills—Agriculture, Defense, Foreign aid, HUD, Military construction, State/Justice/Commerce, and Treasury—the differences between presidential requests and overall congressional appropriations either remained the same or declined; in two other cases—Labor/HEW and Public works—the shift toward "independence" was slight at best. The Interior and Transportation changes were large, but should not necessarily be attributed to budget reform. Indeed, the drop in the Interior mean is largely a function of a single fiscal year (1979); similarly, the discrepancy for Transportation is a result of an extraordinarily large increase in FY 1971.

Table 12–1
Congressional Changes in Presidential Budget Requests, 1966–1979

Fiscal Year	House	Senate	Conference
1966	− 5.6	− 1.2	− 1.8
1967	+ 0.2	− 0.2	− 0.5
1968	− 5.3	− 2.0	− 5.0
1969	− 13.2	− 9.6	− 11.1
1970	− 7.5	− 3.0	− 5.5
1971	− 2.8	− 0.5	− 0.6
1972	− 2.9	− 0.2	− 1.3
1973	− 5.1	− 2.6	− 3.4
1974	− 3.5	− 2.6	− 2.7
1975	− 7.4	− 7.6	− 7.6
1976	− 8.3	− 2.2	− 3.5
1977	− 2.0	− 1.2	− 1.9
1978	− 1.5	− 2.2	− 1.9
1979	− 3.9	− 1.9	− 3.4

Note: Calculated as the differences in percentage changes from the previous year's final total appropriations requested by the president and allowed by the House, Senate, and conference.

Table 12–2
Prereform and Postreform Congressional Changes in Presidential Budget Requests, by Appropriations Bill

Bill	House Prereform	House Postreform	Senate Prereform	Senate Postreform	Conference Prereform	Conference Postreform
Agriculture	− 5.2	− 0.2	+ 5.5	+ 11.2	+ 0.2	+ 0.2
Defense	− 4.1	− 3.2	− 4.4	− 4.1	− 4.3	− 3.9
Foreign aid	− 35.2	− 25.9	− 34.6	− 12.8	− 35.0	− 15.7
HUD	− 6.2	− 9.5	− 1.8	− 1.7	− 4.3	− 11.8
Interior	− 5.1	− 4.4	− 1.0	− 1.8	− 1.6	− 4.4
Labor/HEW	− 3.4	+ 1.2	+ 2.4	+ 1.4	− 0.2	+ 0.4
Military construction	− 23.2	− 11.0	− 22.1	− 5.5	− 22.5	− 8.6
Public works	− 1.8	− 2.2	+ 1.4	− 0.1	− 0.1	− 0.5
State/Justice/ Commerce	− 10.0	− 12.0	− 6.0	+ 4.7	− 5.8	+ 3.0
Transportation	− 9.5	− 7.3	− 3.8	− 2.5	+ 0.6	− 4.5
Treasury	− 5.0	− 1.4	− 1.4	− 0.4	− 2.3	+ 0.1

Note: Mean differences in percentage change from previous year's appropriations requested by the president and allowed by the House, Senate, and conference.

House-Senate Differences. If we calculate the mean differences between House and Senate appropriations for the prereform and postreform periods from the data in table 12–1, we find some support for the second hypothesis. The mean declines from 2.5 in the 1966–1975 period to 1.9 in the 1976–1979 period, a relationship that is depressed by the discrepancy for FY 1976, a year when the reform apparatus was not fully in place (that is, specific allocations from functional budget targets were not made to appropriations subcommittees). The differences for fiscal years 1977, 1978, and 1979 were below all but three of the ten prereform years.

It is instructive to contrast these shifts with changes in individual appropriations bills, however, for as table 12–3 indicates, while the margins of difference have narrowed for some bills, the gap has actually increased for the most of them (though not by very much). Even in that single case where the difference has decreased by almost four points—Labor/HEW—we should not automatically assume that the CBRICA is the cause. The decline in House cuts that produced much of the narrowing in the postreform period in this case coincided with the addition of liberals to the House Labor/HEW appropriations subcommittee; similarly the reduction in Senate increases of this bill do not begin until FY 1978, when a Democratic president began proposing relatively larger Labor/HEW expenditures.

Nor, it should be stressed, are these data obscuring even more fundamental shifts, such as complete House-Senate role reversal. For only two appropriations bills (Defense and Labor/HEW) did the mean Senate cut exceed that of the House in the postreform period. Moreover, if we make pairwise comparisons between all House and Senate appropriations actions for the two periods under consideration, we find that for all bills in the prereform period, Senate appropriations exceeded House appropriations 83 of 108 times (76.9 percent); in the postreform period, the comparable figures are 34 of 55 times (77.2 percent).

Conclusions

Congressional budget reform has been in place too short a time and this study has been too limited in scope to make any final judgments about the full range of the CBRICA's effects. We can say with some surety, however, that there is insufficient evidence to conclude that the 1974 Congressional Budget Reform has fundamentally changed the appropriations process, at least with respect to the two dimensions considered here. Basic prereform appropriations patterns have been carried over into the postreform period. Presidential budget requests appear still to provide the major cues for congressional action; and differentiated House and Senate roles have remained reasonably stable.

Table 12–3
Mean Differences in Absolute Percentages of Presidential Requests
Allowed by the House and Senate, by Appropriations Bill

Bill	Prereform (1966–1975)	Postreform (1976–1979)
Agriculture	10.8	8.7
Defense	0.9	1.0
Foreign aid	9.0	9.1
HUD	3.9	5.4
Interior	3.4	5.7
Labor/HEW	5.0	1.3
Military construction	2.0	5.1
Public works	3.2	1.5
State/Justice/Commerce	4.2	14.9
Transportation	6.7	5.6
Treasury	2.9	1.1

While our judgments about the effects of the CBRICA must be tentative, students of congressional budgeting need to begin to ask whether this reform was not, after all, more symbolism than substance. The CBRICA was born of symbolism, of course. Congress knew that it could never sell the impoundment control provisions it wanted to a president who charged them with fiscal irresponsibility without some effort, however cosmetic, to put its own house in order. Members of Congress who now feel themselves pulled in opposite directions by constituents who want restrained spending, lower taxes, and a balanced budget on the one hand, and increased outlays for all manner of specific programs on the other, may find solace in budget procedures that allow them, apparently, to have both. In the abstract, Congress can pose as a paragon of fiscal responsibility. In specific cases, continued decentralization allows unpleasant choices to be avoided. While time may yet turn symbolism into substance, this is clearly an issue that deserves further research.

Notes

1. Public Law 93–344 (12 July 1974).

2. The most comprehensive treatment is Joel Havemann, *Congress and the Budget* (Bloomington, Ind.: Indiana University Press, 1978). An analysis similar to the one presented in this study has also been done by

Melinda Upp of the Kennedy School at Harvard University, and I am grateful for her assistance in helping to refine some of the ideas discussed here.

3. The CBRICA took effect in FY 1976. Throughout this study, the prereform period refers to fiscal years prior to 1976; postreform refers to fiscal years 1976-1979, inclusive.

4. See Richard F. Fenno, *The Power of the Purse: Appropriations Politics in Congress* (Boston: Little, Brown, 1966).

5. I chose not to include the District of Columbia and legislative appropriations bills in this data set; both are relatively small in size, and the former presents serious problems of standardizing accounts from year to year. Fiscal 1966 is used as a base in this analysis by way of compromise; it is early enough to provide data from the Johnson Administration, which I have used elsewhere to control for partisanship (see my "Training Lobsters to Fly: Assessing the Impacts of the 1974 Congressional Budget Reform," paper presented at the 1979 Annual Meeting of the Midwest Political Science Association), yet is late enough so that it excludes only two appropriations bills (HUD and Transportation for 1966).

6. The annual appropriations summaries prepared by *Congressional Quarterly* are not always consistent across time in terms of the items included in the totals. Wherever necessary (and possible) I standardized the totals by referring to *Congressional Quarterly's* own breakdown of appropriations accounts for each bill.

13 State Tax-Preference Orderings and Partisan Control of Government

Kent E. Portney

Recent research on state policy innovation and enactment of statewide general sales and personal-income taxes has begun to establish the important interaction between fiscal conditions and political systems as determinants of tax policies. However, state tax-policy research ignores the fact that states impose a wide range of taxes, and that the order in which various taxes are preferred differs from state to state. While states undoubtedly enact new taxes in response to fiscal needs and subject to fiscal constraints, the order in which legislatures prefer various taxes may well be subject to a high degree of political choice. This analysis examines the order in which states preferred to adopt three major statewide taxes: the general sales tax; the personal-income tax; and the corporation-income tax. Working from existing analysis, it examines the partisan culture of state politics to help explain preferences among taxes.

Tax Adoptions as Policy Innovation

One area of research attempting to explain policy enactments consists of policy innovation analysis. Several studies of the diffusion of policy innovations among the states have appeared. For example, Jack L. Walker examined eighty-eight different programs adopted by at least twenty states, including establishment of a cigarette tax, a gasoline tax, and a tax commission. Walker constructed an "innovation score" for American states based on elapsed time between the first state adoption of a program and its later adoption by other states.[1] Walker's results indicated that urban, industrialized, and wealthy states were more likely to be innovative. More importantly, Walker suggested that "decision makers are likely to adopt new programs . . . when they become convinced that their state is relatively deprived or that some need exists to which other states in their 'league' have already responded."[2] If research on innovation and diffusion has any relevance for tax policy, it implies that states faced with the perceived need to raise new amounts of revenue will enact new taxes rather than altering existing ones, if they are relatively wealthy and industrialized, and have better educated and more urbanized populations. However, applicability of innovation research in general to the specific area of taxation may not be warranted, since according to Gray, patterns identified by Walker did not necessarily persist for any individual policy area.[3] Nevertheless, patterns of state tax innovation and adoption have received scattered attention.

Patterns of State Tax Adoptions

Recent analyses of state tax enactments have begun to identify some preconditions of new tax adoptions. For example, Berry examined relationships between the party in control of state legislatures and tax adoptions, finding (with many exceptions) that Democrats were more likely to be in control when new taxes were adopted.[4] Hansen expanded this line of analysis, examining patterns of general sales and personal-income tax adoptions from 1911 to 1976.[5] Hansen's analysis focused on the extent to which divided partisan control of state governmental institutions constituted impediments to the enactment of new taxes. In short, she found that less politically competitive states and states with unified partisan control of the legislature and governorship were much more likely to adopt new broad-based taxes, especially in response to economic crises such as the Depression. Even so, it is not clear, given the multiplicity of tax types available to policymakers, why states prefer one tax over others.

Patterns of State Tax Preferences

Even though states experiencing the need for increased revenue in order to respond to extant problems, and experiencing relatively little partisan competition as exhibited in unified partisan control of institutions, are more likely to enact new taxes, patterns of preferences differ. Some states facing these conditions may choose to enact a general sales tax, others might prefer a personal-income tax, and so on. In short, states exhibit a variety of preference orderings for various taxes.

Table 13-1 presents years of enactment for three major state taxes: general sales tax, personal-income tax, and corporation-income tax.[6] This information indicates that as of 1976, 86 percent of the fifty states imposed general sales taxes, 82 percent imposed personal-income taxes, 90 percent imposed corporation-income taxes, and 66 percent imposed all three taxes. Concentrating on dates of enactment for these three major taxes, a state could exhibit any one of thirteen potential preference patterns. Table 13-2 provides the range of possible patterns, along with the number of states exhibiting each pattern. The table indicates, for example, that four states exhibited pattern A, preferring a personal-income tax first, a corporation-income tax second, and a general sales tax third. In some cases, taxes

Table 13–1
Years of Enactment of Personal-Income, General Sales, and Corporation-Income Taxes

State	Year of Personal-Income Tax	Year of General Sales Tax	Year of Corporation-Income Tax
Alabama	1933	1936	1933
Alaska	1949	None	1949
Arizona	1933	1933	1933
Arkansas	1929	1935	1929
California	1935	1933	1929
Colorado	1937	1935	1937
Connecticut	None	1947	1915
Delaware	1917	None	1957
Florida	None	1949	None
Georgia	1929	1951	1929
Hawaii	1901	1935	1901
Idaho	1931	1965	1931
Illinois	1969	1933	1969
Indiana	1963	1963	1963
Iowa	1934	1933	1934
Kansas	1933	1937	1933
Kentucky	1936	1960	1936
Louisiana	1934	1938	1934
Maine	1969	1951	1969
Maryland	1937	1947	1937
Massachusetts	1916	1966	1919
Michigan	1967	1933	1967
Minnesota	1933	1967	1933
Mississippi	1912	1932	1921
Missouri	1917	1934	1917
Montana	1933	None	1917
Nebraska	1967	1967	None
Nevada	None	1955	None
New Hampshire	None	None	1970
New Jersey	1975	1966	1958
New Mexico	1933	1933	1933
New York	1919	1965	1917
North Carolina	1921	1933	1921
North Dakota	1919	1935	1919
Ohio	None	1934	None
Oklahoma	1915	1933	1931
Oregon	1930	None	1929

Table 13-1 continued

State	Year of Personal-Income Tax	Year of General Sales Tax	Year of Corporation-Income Tax
Pennsylvania	1965	1956	1935
Rhode Island	None	None	1947
South Carolina	1922	1951	1922
South Dakota	None	1933	None
Tennessee	None	1947	1923
Texas	None	1961	None
Utah	1931	1933	1931
Vermont	1931	1969	1931
Virginia	1916	1966	1915
Washington	None	None	1933
West Virginia	1961	1933	1967
Wisconsin	1911	1961	1911
Wyoming	None	1935	None

Source: Advisory Commission on Intergovernmental Relations, *State-Local Finances and Suggested Legislation,* 1971 ed., M-57 (Washington, D.C.: ACIR, December 1970), table 23.

characterized as being preferred as a third choice have not yet been enacted.[7] As table 13-2 shows, over a third of the states followed preference pattern H, enacting personal-income and corporation-income taxes together as a first preference, and a general sales tax as a second preference. Another 24 percent exhibited preference pattern G, enacting a general sales tax first, and preferring both a personal-income and a corporation-income tax second. The remaining states exhibited a variety of patterns: 8 percent preferred a personal-income tax first, followed by a corporation-income tax, and a general sales tax; 8 percent preferred a corporation-income tax first, a personal-income tax, then a general sales tax; 10 percent preferred a corporation-income tax first, followed by a general sales tax, and a personal-income tax last. The remaining 14 percent of the states exhibited four different patterns.

While unified partisan control of institutions of government may well facilitate the enactment of new taxes, such control may not, by itself, influence the order of preferences among taxes. However, an examination of tax-preference patterns by the type of traditional partisan control of the legislature and governship reveals that preferences differ according to such institutional constraints. Using the Jewell and Patterson partisan classifications,[8] as shown in table 13-3, half of the traditionally one-party Demo-

Table 13–2
Patterns of Preferences for General Sales, Personal-Income, and
Corporation-Income Taxes in the American States

Type of Tax	Preference Rankings[a]												
	A	B	C	D	E	F	G[b]	H[b]	I[b]	J[b]	K[b]	L[b]	M[b]
Personal-income tax	1	1	2	2	3	3	2	1	1	1	2	2	1
Corporation-income tax	2	3	1	3	1	2	2	1	2	1	1	1	2
General sales tax	3	2	3	1	2	1	1	2	2	1	1	2	1
Number of states	4	0	4	1	5	0	12	18	0	3	0	2	1
Percentage	8	0	8	2	10	0	24	36	0	6	0	4	2

[a] States exhibiting each of the preference patterns are:
A: Delaware, Massachusetts, Mississippi, and Oklahoma.
B: None.
C: Montana, New York, Oregon, and Virginia.
D: West Virginia.
E: California, Connecticut, New Jersey, Pennsylvania, and Tenessee.
F: None.
G. Colorado, Florida, Illinois, Iowa, Maine, Michigan, Nevada, Ohio, South Dakota, Texas, Washington, and Wyoming.
H: Alabama, Alaska, Arkansas, Georgia, Hawaii, Idaho, Kansas, Kentucky, Louisiana, Maryland, Minnesota, Missouri, North Carolina, North Dakota, South Carolina, Utah, Vermont, and Wisconsin.
I: None.
J: Arizona, Indiana, and New Mexico.
K: None.
L: New Hampshire, Rhode Island.
M: Nebraska.
[b] Tied preference rankings occur when two or three taxes were enacted in the same year.

cratic states followed pattern H, preferring a corporation-income tax and a personal-income tax together, followed by a general sales tax. Among the traditonally one-party Republican states, two-thirds exhibited the same performance pattern as one-party Democratic states, pattern H. Moreover, neither the competitive-unified control nor the competitive-divided control states tended to prefer pattern H. Rather, competitive-divided control states preferred a sales tax first, with both the corporation- and personal-income taxes being preferred second. The competitive-divided control states were as likely to exhibit preference pattern E as preference pattern G. Additionally, it would appear that competition is a modest impediment to high preference for taxation of personal incomes. By combining preference patterns A, H, and J, all of which have a personal-income tax as a first preference,[9] this pattern emerges more clearly. As shown in table 13–4, two-thirds of both the one-party Democrat and one-party Republican states enacted personal-income taxes as first preferences. On the other hand, only a third of both the competitive-unified and competitive-divided control states preferred to enact a personal-income tax first.

Competition itself may not directly constitute the impediment to high preference for taxation of personal incomes, since the one-party states may lack sufficient retail sales industries to give a sales tax robust revenue-raising capacity. However, the competitive states are not very likely to prefer a sales tax first, as shown in table 13-4 (by combining categories, D, G, and J).[10] One-party states are extremely likely to prefer a nonsales tax over a sales tax. But only about half of the competitive-unified control states, and only a third of the competitive-divided control states preferred a sales tax first. It does not appear that competitive states give personal-income taxes low priority because of preference for sales taxes, even though noncompetitive states do seem to strongly disfavor sales taxes. Finally, one-party states may prefer personal-income over corporation-income taxes because of the lack of corporate development and resources. Indeed, the one-party Democratic states, most of which are southern, may be expected to possess lower levels of corporation resources to tax. However, as shown in table 13-4, by combining preference categories C, E, H, J, and L,[11] competitive states do not seem to differ from one-party states. It does not appear that competitive states preferred to avoid personal-income taxes because of greater preference for corporation-income taxes.

Summary

While the nature of unified or divided partisan control of the legislature and governorship does not seem to affect preferences for general sales or corporation-income taxes, it does seem to be related to high preference for personal-income taxation. It is likely that one tax is preferred over others for a variety of reasons, including projections of revenue-raising capacity, and predictions of incidence and impact on businesses and industries. However, the results presented here suggest that where there is traditionally a high degree of partisan competitiveness, personal-income taxes are likely to be accorded rather low preferences relative to other taxes. This may well be due to the possibility that personal-income taxes are much more difficult to disguise than other taxes, and in competitive environments, legislators are not likely to risk obvious burdens on constituents.

The need for increased revenue to finance state government is something over which political institutions may well have little influence. Given the perceived need for new taxes, however, political institutions seem to be closely related to the types of broad-based tax chosen. As is normally the case, there are several caveats to the findings presented here. First, the

Table 13–3

Percentage of Distribution of Patterns of Preferences for General Sales, Personal-Income, and Corporation-Income Taxes by Type of Partisan Control of Governorship and Legislature

	Type of Partisan Control of Governorship and Legislature[b]			
Tax Preference Pattern[a]	One-Party Democratic	One-Party Republican	Competitive-Unified Control	Competitive Divided Control
A	12.5	0.0	0.0	16.7
C	6.3	0.0	6.7	16.7
D	6.3	0.0	0.0	0.0
E	6.3	0.0	6.7	25.0
G	12.5	0.0	46.7	25.0
H	50.0	66.7	26.7	8.3
J	6.3	0.0	6.7	8.3
L	0.0	33.3	6.7	0.0
Total	100.0	100.0	100.0	100.0
	N = 16	N = 3	N = 15	N = 12

Note: Excludes Alaska, Hawaii, and nonpartisan Nebraska and Minnesota.

[a] As indicated in table 13–2, patterns B, F, I, K, and M had no cases.

[b] States having each type of partisan control are:

One-party Democratic: Alabama, Arkansas, Arizona, Florida, Georgia, Kentucky, Louisiana, Mississippi, North Carolina, Oklahoma, South Carolina, Tennessee, Texas, Virginia, Maryland, and West Virginia.

One-party Republican: Kansas, New Hampshire, and Vermont.

Competitive-unified control: Idaho, Illinois, Iowa, Maine, Missouri, Michigan, New Jersey, New Mexico, New York, North Dakota, Ohio, Rhode Island, South Dakota, Wisconsin, and Wyoming.

Competitive-divided control: Connecticut, Colorado, Delaware, California, Indiana, Nevada, Massachusetts, Montana, Oregon, Pennsylvania, Utah, and Washington.

analysis focused on the three major statewide taxes, and ignored other sources of revenue, especially various excise taxes. Second, the analysis did not differentiate among sales, personal-income, or corporation-income taxes with regard to rates and rate structures. Finally, the analysis did not seek to discover alternative political process explanations for various tax preferences. For example, state legislatures that were historically malapportioned to favor rural interests may have favored taxation of relatively higher urban personal incomes over other forms of taxation. It does seem clear, however, that states lacking a high degree of partisan competitiveness show a marked tendency to accord a high preference to taxation of personal incomes relative to other types of taxes.

Table 13-4
Percentage of Distribution of First Preferences for Personal-Income, General Sales, and Corporation-Income Taxes by Type of Partisan Control

Tax Preference Pattern	Type of Partisan Control of Governorship and Legislature [a]			
	One-Party Democratic	One-Party Republican	Competitive-Unified Control	Competitive-Divided Control
Personal-income tax is first preference (patterns A,H,J)	68.8	66.7	33.3	33.3
Personal-income tax is not first preference (all other patterns)	31.2	33.3	66.7	66.7
Totals	100.0	100.0	100.0	100.0
	$N = 16$	$N = 3$	$N = 15$	$N = 12$
Cramer's V = .35 contingency coefficient = .33				
General sales tax is first preference (patterns D,G,J)	25.0	0.0	53.3	33.3
General sales tax is not first preference (all other patterns)	75.0	100.0	46.7	66.7
Totals	100.0	100.0	100.0	100.0
	$N = 16$	$N = 3$	$N = 15$	$N = 12$
Cramer's V = .31 contingency coefficient = .30				
Corporation-income tax is first preference (patterns C,E,H,J,L)	68.7	100.0	53.3	58.3
Corporation-income tax is not first preference (all other patterns)	31.3	0.0	46.7	41.7
Totals	100.0	100.0	100.0	100.0
	$N = 16$	$N = 3$	$N = 15$	$N = 12$
Cramer's V = .24 contingency coefficient = .24				

Note: Excludes Alaska, Hawaii, and nonpartisan Nebraska and Minnesota.
[a] See note b, table 13.3 for partisan classifications.

Notes

1. Jack L. Walker, "The Diffusion of Innovations among the American States," *American Political Science Review* 63 (September 1969):880–899.
2. Ibid., p. 897.

3. Virginia Gray, "Innovations in the States: A Diffusion Study," *American Political Science Review* 67 (December 1973):1174–1185.

4. Frances Berry, "Taxation in the American States: A Comparative Study of Diffusion and Innovation" (Master's thesis, University of Minnesota, 1967).

5. Susan B. Hansen, "The Politics of State Tax Innovation," (paper delivered at the 1978 Annual Meetings of the Midwest Political Association, 20–22 April 1978).

6. These taxes are used because of their importance as sources of state revenue. In 1976, the general sales tax accounted for 30.6 percent of total state-tax collections, the personal-income tax accounted for 24 percent, and the corporation-income tax, 8.1 percent.

7. For example, the state of Delaware exhibited pattern A, enacting a personal-income tax first and a corporation-income tax second. Delaware had no general sales tax, and the sales tax was considered to be the third preference of the state among the three taxes.

8. Malcolm E. Jewell and Samuel C. Patterson, *The Legislative Process in the United States* (New York: Random House, 1966), pp. 143–144. Competitive-unified states are defined as states where the same party controlled both houses of the legislature from 1947 to 1966 and usually the governorship. Competitive-divided control states are defined as two-party states where no single party had dominant legislative control.

9. As shown in table 13–2, preference patterns B and I also called for personal-income tax as first preference. However, no states exhibited these patterns.

10. As shown in table 13–2, preference patterns F and K also called for a general sales tax first. However, no states exhibited these patterns.

11. Preference pattern K also called for a corporation-income tax as first preference. However, no states exhibited this pattern.

14 The Determinants of Individual Tax Preferences: A Public-Choice Analysis

Margaret McKay

Over the past thirty years, the debate surrounding the relative impact of socioeconomic and political variables on public-policy outcomes has produced a body of literature that still remains salient.[1] The early theoretical contribution of Key and Lockard[2] suggested that quantitative models relying on aggregate data could assess the relative impact of environmental variables on public-policy decisions. Although the empirical debate is far from a satisfactory resolution, adversarial lines can be drawn along three dimensions: (1) the choice and operationalization of independent variables (social, economic, and political),[3] (2) the choice of dependent variable (redistributive, and incremental policies),[4] and (3) the choice of methodology (simple and partial correlation, multiple regression, and path and factor analysis).[5]

Without seeming to ignore the existence and dimensions of the determinants debate, this study seeks to circumvent the policy-impact question by focusing instead on identifying the determinants of individual's tax preferences. Implicit in this focus is the assumption that, in some manner, individual preferences are related ultimately to policy decisions.[6]

The purpose of this research is to identify the factors that contribute to a person's decision-making calculus with respect to three alternative taxes—income, sales, and property—and the relative influence of each in the taxpayer's final preference. The analytical model adopted for this investigation is the public-choice model. In its simplest form, it is a variant of the market model in which the basic postulate is that man is an "egoistic, rational, utility maximizer."[7]

In recent years the model has gained considerable currency among scholars through its application to voting behavior, particularly behavior related to taxing and spending measures.[8] Under these conditions, the voters are viewed as consumer-taxpayers and are expected to demonstrate rationality in their voting patterns. Rationality is almost always defined in terms of the narrow, short-run, means-ends relationships.[9] Like the consumer, the taxpayer's objective is to exchange a price (tax dollar) for a product (public service). The taxpayer's willingness to pay the price is dependent on the value he or she places on the particular service involved.

Inasmuch as public services are seldom distributed according to price,[10] taxpayers are unable to develop a cost-benefit calculus capable of determining its utility maximizing effect. However, there is some evidence to suggest that taxpayers view the tax price independent of the tax benefit.[11] To the extent that this is true, people's tax preferences will more accurately reflect perceptions of their short-run, personal, economic self-interest without regard to the benefits associated with the tax.[12] This condition becomes more pronounced in light of the current tendency to rely more on indirect forms of taxation.[13]

In analyzing consumer-taxpayer behavior, the public-choice model's most serious weakness is its bias favoring quantifiable (economic) factors.[14] It becomes a more serious concern when the issue under examination encompasses a variety of noneconomic variables (for example, social, political, and psychological). Buchanan suggested, however, that the utility of the consumer-taxpayer model increases when the alternative "means" relative to a specific goal can be defined in economic terms.[15] Under certain conditions, therefore, economic motivation concerning political decisions has proved sufficiently dominant to permit hypothesis testing against actual observable behavior.[16]

The assumptions of this study are: (1) individuals are capable of calculating the direct short-term consequences of alternative tax choices, (2) they are capable of assessing and rating these consequences according to their perceptions of their self-interest, and (3) the results of these calculations will be reflected in their stated tax preferences.

The environment under investigation closely approximates the conditions suggested by Buchanan. To correct the state's interschool-district fiscal disparities, the New Jersey Supreme Court had mandated, in effect, a substantial alteration of the state's existing tax structure.[17] Since the structures were incapable of generating sufficient revenues to accomplish this task,[18] the state was compelled to expand its existing tax instruments or to create new ones. Several years of study by the New Jersey Tax Policy Commission has produced a number of suggestions for reform among which were (1) a state income tax, (2) an increased sales tax, and (3) a statewide property tax.[19]

At the time of this research, the property tax was virtually the exclusive taxing instrument of local governments.[20] The sales tax, having been in existence for eight years, was set at 5 percent.[21] The state had no income tax.[22] On several occasions an income-tax bill had been debated in the state legislature and overwhelmingly defeated.[23] But in the spring of 1974, an income-tax bill failed in the lower house by a margin of only three votes.[24] Both in the news media and in the legislative chambers, discussion and controversy surrounding the income-tax question reached a highly emotional level. It was during this turbulent period that this research was conducted.

Research Design and Procedures

The basic unit of analysis is the individual. The research objective is to identify and assess the relative influence of the factors that contribute to individual tax preferences. The general hypothesis is that individuals will rate their tax preferences according to their economic self-interest.

One of the most critical elements of the public-choice model is the assumption that individuals possess considerable knowledge concerning the cost-benefit ratio associated with a given tax-spending trade-off. For this reason, a survey of the general population was rejected in favor of one consisting of local school board members because of the latter's greater awareness of school finance affairs.

Surveying school board members has an additional advantage. Congressional and state assembly districts overlap a number of school districts. This condition creates ambiguities in developing a cost-benefit calculus with respect to a prospective tax-reform measure. School districts, on the other hand, have a tax base (assessed valuation) that is directly related to the financing of public schools within their jurisdiction. It is assumed, therefore, that the economic consequences of a tax measure created specifically for this purpose will be more clearly discernible by school board members than by representatives of other governmental entities.[25]

Dependent Variables

The data are derived from a cross-sectional analysis of individual responses to a mail questionnaire sent to a stratified sample of New Jersey school board members.[26] The primary objective is to determine the relationship between an individual's economic self-interest and his or her tax preferences. The dependent variables are the respondents' rating of three alternative taxes: income, sales, and statewide property.

Economic Variables

In an effort to determine whether the respondents' tax preferences reflect their own personal self-interest or (acting in the capacity of an elected representative) those of their constituency, two measures of economic self-interest are employed for each tax. The indicator of economic self-interest most frequently used in studies such as this is personal or family income. The measures used here are a function of the particular tax under investigation.

The respondent's personal economic self-interest is measured in terms of his or her family income. Among many taxpayers there is a generalized notion that the income tax is progressive and the sales tax is regressive.[27] Based on this assumption, wealthy people are expected to oppose the income tax and less affluent people, to favor it. The hypothesis is: personal income will be inversely related to income-tax preferences. Similar reasoning applies to the board member's school district's self-interest, measured in terms of the district's median family income.[28] The hypothesis is: median family income will be inversely related to income-tax preferences. The hypotheses for sales-tax preferences are: personal income will be positively related to sales-tax preferences, and median income will be positively related to sales-tax preferences.

The economic effects of a statewide property tax would be that districts with high-tax rates, usually poor ones, would experience a tax reduction without a concomitant loss of total revenue.[29] Districts with low-tax rates would realize a rate increase accompanied, most likely, by a revenue loss.[30]

Since the statewide property tax affects jurisdictional or public wealth, not necessarily individual or private wealth, the conceptual link between this tax and the board member's personal self-interest is ambiguous. In spite of this ambiguity, a pattern is anticipated. People may perceive the adoption of a statewide property tax as a shift toward greater reliance on the property tax generally and a greater increase in their tax burden specifically. With this thought in mind, the hypothesis is: the value of a board member's home will be inversely related to statewide property-tax preferences. No ambiguities exist with respect to the link between statewide property tax and a district's economic self-interest. Poor districts will tend to benefit from it: rich ones will not. The school district's wealth is measured in terms of its tax base (per pupil assessed valuation).[31] The hypothesis is: the wealth of a school district will be inversely related to statewide property-tax preferences.

Political Variables

In attempting to establish statistical relationships, it is frequently the case that all things are never equal. It becomes necessary, therefore, to identify factors other than economic self-interest that are likely to influence individuals' tax preferences. Much of the existing research findings indicate that some measure of economic self-interest plays a significant role in predicting individual tax preferences.[32] The findings also suggest that partisanship, age, education, and (rural-urban) residency influence them as well.[33] According to several studies, Democrats tend to favor the income tax and oppose the sales tax. Conversely, Republicans tend to favor the sales tax and oppose the income tax.[34] While the findings concerning the influence of partisanship on property tax are inconsistent, in this study Democrats are expected to favor the statewide property tax (Republicans oppose it) because of its equalization effect.

Although numerous studies have been conducted on the influence of ideology on political elites generally,[35] no research endeavor thus far has sought to examine its role in determining individual tax preferences. One of the reasons for this omission is the methodological problems encountered with respect to identification, measurement, and interpretation of data.[36] The problems are significantly reduced when measurement indicators rely on the self-classification system.[37] School board members indicated on a continuum labeled "very liberal" to "very conservative" the position that most accurately reflects their orientation with respect to state and local issues. The anticipated relationship is that liberalism will be positively related to income-tax preferences and negatively related to sales-tax preferences. Conservatism is expected to reveal a reverse pattern.

Sociodemographic Variables

The findings concerning the relationship of age to income and sales-tax preferences are contradictory.[38] Because of the close association of age to income, it seems logical to expect age to be negatively related to income tax and positively related to sales-tax preferences. The findings show, however, that support for the property tax declines as age increases. Age, therefore, is expected to be negatively related to statewide property-tax preferences.

With respect to the influence of education on tax preferences, the findings are also inconsistent. The data seem to suggest that the level of education is positively related to people's attitude concerning the proper size of the public sector.[39] Education, therefore, is expected to be positively related to income and sales-tax and negatively related to statewide property-tax preferences.

The influence of residency location on tax preferences is fairly consistent. Urban residents tend to favor the income tax and oppose the sales and property tax: rural residents reveal a reverse pattern.[40] New Jersey school board members are expected to reflect this tendency.

Research Methodology

The statistical model initially adopted was stepwise multiple regression. The R^2 provided less than 6 percent of the explanation of total variance.[41] As an alternative procedure, cross-tabulation matrices, relying on bivariate analysis, were created. The data are contained in tables 14–1, 14–2, and 14–3.

Table 14–1
The Self-Interest Variable

Independent Variables Self-Interest	Tax Preferences (percentage of support)			
	Income	Sales	Property	N
Personal income				
Under $12,000	36 [a]	26	7	42
$12,000–$20,000	48	16	17	174
$21,000–$30,000	50	17	17	143
Over $30,000	55	21	17	125
District median income				
Low	42	22 [b]	19	170
Medium	50	15	18	166
High	55	16	14	178
Home value				
Low	—	—	17	94
Medium	—	—	18	156
High	—	—	17	127
District wealth				
Low	—	—	18	170
Medium	—	—	15	162
High	—	—	17	182

Significance: [a] = .02, [b] = .05.

Table 14–2
Political Variables

Independent Variables Political Variables	Tax Preferences (percentage of support)			
	Income	Sales	Property	N
Partisanship				
Democrat	57 [a]	14	15	124
Republican	42	23	18	173
Independent	52	16	16	197
Ideology				
Liberal	62 [b]	9 [b]	19	144
Moderate	46	22	12	167
Conservative	45	18	20	188

Significance: [a] = .0009, [b] = .003.

Research Findings

The least satisfactory aspect of this study was the failure to obtain statistical significance among many of the cross-tabulation matrices. Only ten of the

Table 14–3
Social and Life-style Characteristics

Independent Variables Social factors	Tax Preferences (percentage of support)			
	Income	Sales	Property	N
Age				
Under 30	54	8	15	26
30–45 years	45	16	20	206
46–60 years	51	18	18	148
Over 60	36	29	7	28
Education				
Less-than high school	42	25[a]	—	12
High-school graduate	46	17	—	195
College	52	18	—	301
Life-style				
Area				
Rural	36[a]	24	18	90
Suburban	52	17	17	292
Urban	52	16	15	131

Significance: [a] = .04.

hypotheses produced significant data, none of them were associated with statewide property-tax preferences. The data in table 14–1 demonstrate that the explanatory properties of economic self-interest, measured in terms of personal income, are limited to income-tax preferences only. Moreover, the patterns are contrary to what was anticipated at the outset of this study by revealing a clear and consistently positive relationship between personal income and income-tax preferences. That is, as income rises, the likelihood increases that people will prefer the income tax. The data relying on constituent measures of self-interest also contradict the hypotheses by revealing a negative and positive effect on sales-tax and income-tax preferences, respectively. The findings for statewide property tax, while statistically insignificant, are also inconsistent with respect to the direction of the influence.

Political Variables

The hypotheses concerning partisanship are partly validated by the data. Table 14–2 shows that Democrats do indeed favor the income tax more than do Republicans. Moreover, they favor this tax by a margin of 33 percent over the sales tax. While Republicans show less support for the income tax and more support for the sales tax than do Democrats, they also showed more support than opposition to the income tax. (Actual opposition of Republicans to the income and sales tax was 34 percent and 33 percent, respectively, not included in table 14–2.)

Of all the variables examined, ideology demonstrates the most significant and consistent pattern of influence on both income-tax and sales-tax preferences. The data in table 14–2 confirm the hypotheses. Liberals clearly favor the income tax by 17 percent over conservatives. Similarly, conservatives favor the sales tax, but by only nine percentage points over liberals.

Sociodemographic Variables

The influence of age on tax preferences shown in table 14–3 partly refutes the expected pattern. Age is positively related to income-tax and sales-tax support and negatively related to statewide property-tax support. The data also show that the influence of education on tax preferences is statistically significant only for sales-tax preferences. The influence of higher education on sales-tax preferences appears to be negative, with college graduates demonstrating the least support. It should be noted, however, that only a very small percentage of the population sample had less than a high school education. The relationship, therefore, while statistically significant, may not be very meaningful.

The anticipated support pattern for urban-rural residency is confirmed for income and sales tax and inconclusive for statewide property-tax preferences. Table 14–3 shows that urban residents favor the income tax and oppose the sales tax more than do their rural neighbors by a margin of 16 and 8 percent, respectively. Suburban board members have preferences similar to those in urban areas.

Conclusion

In an abbreviated form, the hypotheses appear in table 14–4. Each independent variable and its related dependent variable is listed together with its anticipated and actual relationship. The data provide evidence that conventional indicators of economic self-interest are not the dominant influence of people's tax preferences. Furthermore, the influence they do exert is opposite to what we would normally expect. Noneconomic factors appear to play a more influential role in taxpayer psychology. The dominant influence of political ideology and party affiliation, for example, appears to confirm the suggestion made by Key and Downs whereby both factors function as shortcut decision-making mechanisms with respect to political behavior.[42]

Table 14–4
Abbreviated Summary of Hypotheses and Findings

Independent Variable	Anticipated Relationship	Dependent Variable (tax preferences)	Findings
1. Personal income	Negative	Income tax	Refuted
2. Median income	Negative	Income tax	Refuted
3. Personal income	Positive	Sales tax	Refuted
4. Median Income	Positive	Sales tax	Refuted
5. Own home (value)	Negative	Statewide property tax	Not supported
6. District wealth	Negative	Statewide property tax	Not supported
7. Democrat	Positive	Income tax	Supported
8. Democrat	Negative	Sales tax	Supported
9. Republican	Negative	Income tax	Partly supported
10. Republican	Positive	Sales tax	Partly supported
11. Liberal	Positive	Income tax	Supported
12. Liberal	Positive	Statewide property tax	Not supported
13. Liberal	Negative	Sales tax	Supported
14. Conservative	Negative	Income tax	Partly supported
15. Conservative	Negative	Statewide property tax	Not supported
16. Conservative	Positive	Sales tax	Partly supported
17. Age	Negative	Sales tax	Refuted
18. Age	Negative	Statewide property tax	Not supported
19. Education	Positive	Income tax	Supported
20. Urban	Positive	Income tax	Supported
21. Urban	Negative	Sales tax	Supported
22. Urban	Negative	Statewide property tax	Supported
23. Rural	Negative	Income tax	Partly supported
24. Rural	Positive	Sales tax	Partly supported
25. Rural	Positive	Statewide property tax	Partly supported

Policy Implications of Findings

By relying on survey data of school board members, this study suggests that they might properly serve as surrogates for two other groups. First, they are taxpayers who, by virtue of their specialized role, possess expertise concerning the nature of school finance. Their tax-preference patterns may reflect those of taxpayers in their local communities.[43] Second, they are also legislators and policymakers. In this capacity, they are representatives of constituency interests.[44] Their tax preferences, therefore, may serve as indirect indicators of state legislators' preferences acting in a similar capacity. Given the current impetus for school tax reform that has been generated by the numerous Serrano-type decisions,[45] the tax-preference patterns of school board members may serve as a harbinger of tax-reform policies in state legislatures in New Jersey and elsewhere.[46]

The policymaking question to which this research effort addresses itself is: will state legislators, when faced with the issue of school finance reform, make decisions that reflect their own personal economic self-interest or their constituency's self-interest, or will their decisions reflect the influence of noneconomic factors? The findings of this study suggest that economic considerations are less influential in these kinds of decisions than conventional wisdom or existing research findings would indicate. They show that other factors, such as political ideology, partisanship, life-style, and possibly some vague notion of "publicness," have a greater influence on decisions concerning public finance.[47]

Notes

1. For one of the most recent summaries of the determinants literature see Michael S. Lewis-Beck, "The Relative Importance of Socioeconomic and Political Variables for Public Policy," *American Political Science Review* 71, no. 2 (June 1977): 559–566.

2. V.O. Key, Jr., *Southern Politics* (New York: Vintage Books, 1949), p. 307; Duane Lockard, *New England State Politics* (Princeton, N.J.: Princeton University Press, 1959), pp. 320–340.

3. Michael S. Lewis-Beck and Lawrence B. Mohr, "Evaluating Effects of Independent Variables," *Political Methodology* 3 (February 1976): 27–47.

4. Terry N. Clark, "Community Social Indicators: From Analytical Model to Policy," *Urban Affairs Quarterly* 9, no. 1 (September 1973): 3–36.

5. Lewis-Beck, "Socioeconomic and Political Variables."

6. V.O. Key, Jr., *Public Opinion and American Democracy* (New York: Alfred A. Knopf, 1963), pp. 442–443; Anthony Downs, *An Economic Theory of Democracy* (New York: Harper and Row, 1957), p. 98.

7. For a thorough discussion of the public-choice model and its theoretical assumptions see Dennis C. Mueller, "Public Choice: A Survey," *Journal of Economic Literature* 14, no. 2 (June 1976): 395–433.

8. One of the earliest studies devoted to this subject is James Q. Wilson and Edward C. Banfield, "Voting Behavior on Municipal Public Expenditures: A Study in Rationality and Self-Interest," in *The Public Economy of Urban Communities,* ed. Jules Margolis (Baltimore: Johns Hopkins Press, 1965), pp. 74–91. For more recent studies that focus on

using the public-choice model for tax measures, see Richard L. Lucier, "The Prediction of Public Choice Behavior in the Washington Tax Substitution Referendum," *National Tax Journal* 26, no. 4 (December 1973): 625–630, and Donna E. Shalala, Mary F. Williams, and Andrew Fishel, *The Property Tax and the Voters: An Analysis of State Constitutional Referenda to Revise School Finance Systems in California, Colorado, Michigan, and Oregon in 1972 and 1973* (New York: Institute of Philosophy and Politics of Education, Teachers College, Columbia University) occational paper no. 2, 1973.

9. Kenneth Arrow, *Social Choice and Individual Values* (New York: John Wiley and Sons, 1951), p. 7.

10. Gierhand Colm, *Essays in Public Finance and Fiscal Policy* (New York: Oxford University Press, 1955), p. 32.

11. James Buchanan, *Public Finance in Democratic Process* (North Carolina: University of North Carolina Press, 1967), pp. 88–95.

12. Colm, *Essays in Public Finance.*

13. Shlomo Maital, "Preferences, Tax Structure and Tax Reform: Theory and Evidence," *Public Finance Quarterly* 3, no. 1 (January 1975): 361–382.

14. The most comprehensive critique of applying the public-choice model to political phenomena is Thomas Conrad's "Rationality and Political Science," *Polity* 2, no. 4 (Summer 1970): 479–493.

15. Buchanan, *Public Finance,* p. 118.

16. In his article, "Budgets and Ballots: The Political Consequences of Fiscal Choice," Theodore Eismeier demonstrates the positive relationship between the incidence of statutory rises in state taxes and the subsequent electoral defeat of governors (unpublished paper delivered at the 1978 annual meeting of the Midwest Political Science Association, Chicago, Illinois, April 19–22, 1978).

17. *Robinson* v. *Cahill,* 62 N.J. 473 (1973).

18. *New Jersey Tax Policy Commission, Summary Report* (Trenton, New Jersey: State of New Jersey, 1972), p. 2.

19. *Ibid.*

20. *Ibid.*

21. *New Jersey Department of Treasury, Annual Report of the Division of Taxation for Fiscal Year 1974* (Trenton, New Jersey: State of New Jersey, 1975).

22. In point of fact, New Jersey had a limited income tax in 1974 which was levied on income earned outside the state by residents of New Jersey and income earned within the state by nonresidents. It was called a transportation tax and was levied primarily on income earned by residents of New York and Pennsylvania. Tax revenues are used to defray transportation costs from New Jersey to the other two states. The state waives the tax

for people who pay an income tax in their respective states. Revenues from this tax amounted to less than 8 percent of the state's total tax collections in 1974. *Annual Report,* pp. 80–83.

23. Jerome Zukosky, "No to Tax Reform: Failure in New Jersey," *The New Republic,* 5 and 12 August 1972.

24. *The New York Times,* 16 April 1974, p. 1.

25. School districts and school boards have been the focus of numerous empirical studies because they possess a variety of other characteristics that lend themselves readily to comparative research. Among these are their (1) relative small size, (2) distinct fiscal jurisdiction, (3) intradistrict social and economic homogeneity, and (4) intrastate social and economic heterogeneity. Also they are perhaps the last bastion of local control. For example, see Basil G. Zimmer and Amos H. Hawley, "Opinions on School District Reorganization in Metropolitan Areas: A Comparative Analysis of the Views of Citizens and Officials in Central City and Suburban Areas," *The Southwestern Social Science Quarterly* 48, no. 3 (December 1967): 311–325; M. Kent Jennings and Harmon Zeigler, "Response Styles and Politics: The Case of School Boards," *Midwest Journal of Political Science* 15, no. 2 (May 1971): 290–321; and Peter J. Cistone and Bernard Hennessy, "School Board Members' Attitudes and Administrative Forms: An Exploration of Public Regardingness," *Midwest Journal of Political Science* 15, no. 4, (August 1971): 587–594.

26. The total adjusted number of school boards (582) were classified into urban, suburban, and rural categories according to an "urban" index created specifically for this study. The index incorporated the density factor with geographic proximity to the nearest SMSA such that 8.6 percent of the districts were urban, 51 percent were suburban, and 40 percent were rural.

27. This assumption does not mean to ignore the current debate concerning the progressive-regressive nature of the property and income tax. For this study, however, it is assumed that most people perceive the property tax as regressive and the income tax as progressive. (That is, to the extent that they have any perceptions of tax incidence at all.) Their attitudes therefore, will reflect these perceptions, not necessarily the reality of the tax world. For one of the earliest challenges to traditional regressive position on property taxes, see Mason Gaffney, "The Property Tax Is a Progressive Tax," *Proceedings of the 64th Annual Conference, National Tax Association* (1971): 408–426. For a brief summary of the incidence studies up to 1974, see Henry Aaron's, *Who Pays the Property Tax?* (Washington, D.C.: Brookings Institution, 1975), pp. 25–27. Also for more recent treatment that refutes the progressive position, see David E. Black, "Property Tax Incidence: The Excise-Tax Effect and Assessment Practices," *National Tax Journal* 30, no. 4 (December 1977): 429–434.

28. U.S. Department of Commerce, Bureau of the Census, New Jersey, 1970.

29. For a discussion of the consequences of state equalization formulas, see Joel S. Berke, *Answers to Inequity: An Analysis of the New School Finance* (Berkeley, Calif.: McCutchan Publishing Corp., 1974), p. 112. There is considerable debate concerning the fiscal consequences of equalization techniques. For example, see "A Statistical Analysis of the School Finance Decisions: On Winning Battles and Losing Wars," *The Yale Law Journal* 81 (1972): 27-41.

30. This conclusion rests on the assumption that an inverse relationship exists between a school district's property-tax rate and the wealth of the district's tax base. While this assumption may not be valid for other states, it is for New Jersey. Six of the poorest districts in the state had tax rates well above the average: Hoboken ($3,680—6.98 percent), Newark ($4,061—6.46 percent), Orange ($5,067—7.22 percent), Camden ($3,608—5.95 percent), Trenton ($3,832—6.12 percent), and Jersey City ($4,414—5.62 percent). The state average per pupil assessed valuation in 1973 was $54,470 and the average tax rate was 2.72 percent. *Twenty-second Annual Report.* Also see Margaret M. McKay, "The Urban Fiscal Paradox: An Experience in Reality Testing" (unpublished manuscript, 1976).

31. *Twenty-second Annual Report.*

32. H. Cantrill, *Public Opinion, 1935-1946* (Princeton, N.J.: Princeton University Press, 1951), pp. 325-326; Elizabeth L. David, "Public Preferences and the Tax Structure" (Ph.D. diss., University of Michigan, 1961); Leon D. Epstein, *Votes and Taxes* (Madison, Wis.: University of Wisconsin Institute of Governmental Affairs, 1964); Elizabeth L. David, "A Comparative Study of Tax Preferences," *National Tax Journal* 20, no. 1 (January 1967): 98-101; Meltzner, pp. 224-247; "Taxes and Services: New City Revenue Sources Favored," *Nation's Cities* (August 1991): 12-16; William Watts and Lloyd Free, eds., *State of the Nation* (Washington, D.C.: Potomac Associates, 1973), pp. 347-348; Floyd J. Fowler, Jr., *Citizen Attitudes toward Local Government Services and Taxes* (Cambridge, Mass.: Ballinger Publishing Co., 1976), pp. 57-67; Advisory Commission on Intergovernmental Relations, *Public Opinion and Taxes* (Washington, D.C.: Government Printing Office, 1972); ACIR, *Changing Public Attitudes on Governments and Taxes,* 1976, and idem, *Changing Public Attitudes on Governments and Taxes,* 1977.

33. ACIR, *Public Attitudes,* 1977.

34. Epstein, *Votes and Taxes,* p. 17; David, "Public Preferences," p. 50.

35. David Minar, "Ideology and Political Behavior," *Midwest Journal of Political Science* 5, no. 4 (November 1961): 317-331; Herman McClosky,

Paul J. Hoffman, and Rosemary O'Hara, "Issues, Conflict and Consensus among Party Leaders," *American Political Science Review* 14, no. 2 (June 1960): 406–427; idem, "Consensus and Ideology in American Politics," *American Political Science Review* 63, no. 2 (June 1964): 361–382; Philip Converse, "The Nature of Belief Systems in Mass Publics," in *Ideology and Discontent,* ed. David Apter (Glencoe, N.Y.: Free Press, 1964).

36. Jeff Fishell, "Party Ideology and the Congressional Challenger," *American Political Science Review* 63, no. 4 (December 1969): 1213–1232, 1216.

37. Ibid.; Douglas E. Mitchell, "Ideological Structures and School Policy-Making," (Ph.D. diss., Claremont Graduate School, 1972), p. 258.

38. ACIR, *Public Attitudes,* 1977.

39. David, "Public Preferences," p. 29; "Taxes and Services."

40. ACIR, *Public Attitudes,* 1977.

41. The R^2s for each tax preference were income tax, $R^2 = .056$, sales tax, $R^2 = .044$, and statewide property tax, $R^2 = .046$.

42. Key, *Public Opinion,* pp. 442–443; Downs, *Economic Theory,* p. 98.

43. Meltzner, pp. 248–285.

44. The existing research findings indicate that certain policy areas provide more decision-making latitude in legislative voting than do other areas. See Warren E. Miller and Donald E. Stokes, "Constituency Influence in Congress," *American Political Science Review* 62, no. 1 (March 1963): 45–56. There is no evidence so far, however, that indicates that tax policy is among the areas where wide latitude exists.

45. *Serrano* v. *Priest et al.,* 5 Cal. 3d 584, 487 P. 2d 1241, 96 Cal. Rptr. 601 (1971). The landmark California decision ruled that the state's heavy reliance on the wealth of a school district resulted in a wide discrepancy in the quality of education and therefore violated the equal-protection clause of the state's and United States' constitutions. Even though the U.S. Supreme Court subsequently overturned a similar Texas case (*San Antonio Independent School District* v. *Rodrigues,* 411 M.S. 1, 1973), less than two years after Serrano over thirty states had followed California's lead. *Analysis of Interstate School Finance Cases* (Washington, D.C.: U.S. Office of Education, Department of Health, Education and Welfare, 1972).

46. In point of historical fact, New Jersey adopted an income-tax measure in 1976, ACIR, *Significant Features of Fiscal Federalism* 2, Revenue and Department, 1976–1977 (Washington, D.C.: March 1977).

47. One of the earliest empirical studies of "publicness" was conducted by James Q. Wilson and Edward C. Banfield, "Public Regardingness as a Value Premise in Voting Behavior," *American Political Science Review* 53 (December 1964): 876–887.

15 Explaining Michigan's Vote on the Tisch Amendment

David Lowery

The tax revolt should be of obvious concern to those interested in state and local government. The revolt threatens the local provision of public services as restricted revenues lead to service cutbacks or their being shifted to other levels of government.[1] The revolt may even be indicative of a breakdown in local representative government; the tax and expenditure decisions of elected representatives are being rejected. Also the tax revolt is more than a California issue. Tax limits or tax cuts have been adopted by twenty-four states since California's adoption of Proposition 13.

But despite the potential of the tax revolt to reshape local government, there has been little effort to explain why it is occurring. Most of the literature on the tax revolt concerns administrative responses to revenue shortages under the heading of cutback management. While important, examination of this issue says little or nothing about the causes of the tax revolt. A second set of literature has used California voting data to interpret voter objectives on Proposition 13.[2] This work is primarily descriptive and unconnected to any broader theoretic understanding of public production processes; it is at best only indirectly useful in explaining the causes of the tax revolt.[3] Two recent examinations of the tax revolt in Michigan have made a partial step in that direction.[4] Unfortunately, they too are limited as their narrowly focused models are tested in isolation from any alternative explanations of the tax revolt, and the empirical results are inconclusive or have yet to be presented.[5] Little progress has been made in explaining the tax revolt. More importantly, no research program has emerged which could serve as a guide for progressive theory development on the tax revolt.

This study is a preliminary attempt to identify and test several alternative approaches to understanding the tax revolt. In the first section, several candidate explanations of the tax revolt are presented. Two of the models represent the dominant approaches to understanding public-sector production: the median-voter and excessive-government models. This is followed by a test using ordinary least squares (OLS) regression with cross-sectional data on Michigan municipalities. Data on Michigan's recent Tisch amendment referendum is used to measure the level of support for the tax revolt. The Tisch amendment was very similar to California's Proposition 13 and would have cut property taxes in half had it passed. In the final section, the implications of the findings of the study of the tax revolt are discussed.

Explaining the Tax Revolt

Before examining the tax revolt, it may prove useful to identify the conditions under which the revolt would not occur: the Tiebout model. The
Tiebout model posits a local public-goods market analogous to the private
goods market where, in Tiebout's words, "the consumer voter moves to
that community whose local government best satisfies his set of prefences.
The greater number of communities and the greater variance among
them, the closer the consumer will come to fully realizing his preference
position."[6] The result of the revenue- and expenditure-derived locational
decisions is a set of communities with intracommunity identical household public-goods demand producing an optimal level of public-goods
provision.

Of course, the Tiebout model has limited descriptive value given its
restrictive assumptions on information, mobility, and externalities. Pack
and Pack demonstrated that locational decisions are not determined by the
level of public-goods provision and that there is considerable intracommunity variance in the level of public-goods demand. But the Tiebout model is
still important because it provides a baseline against which to analyze the
occurrence of the tax revolt. As Pack and Pack suggested, "In a Tiebout . .
world such initiatives (as Proposition 13)[7] would be very surprising."[8] In a
pure Tiebout world, each household would find the local tax-expenditure
decision to be optimal making a tax revolt unthinkable. Additionally, for
better or worse, the Tiebout model has assumed a normative value in public-
choice theory. The model provides for complete preference revelation and a
broad range of consumer-voter choice. As we will see later, this has some
interesting implications for evaluating the various candidate explanations of
the tax revolt. Given that we do not live in a Tiebout-like world, how are we
to explain the tax revolt? Three potential explanations are discussed below.

Revolt by the Minority: The Median-Voter Model

In a non-Tiebout world, some mechanism other than locational decisions is
needed to produce a tolerable tax-expenditure decision. The median-voter
model suggests that the political process employs issue position movement
by the political entrepreneur to achieve a satisfactory if nonoptimal result.
Assuming that demands for public goods are distributed on a continuum,
the model demonstrates that politicians who adopt platforms conforming to
the preferences of the median voter will achieve electoral success. Platforms
based on a nonmedian strategy would fail to produce majority support.
Tax-expenditure decisions in a perfect median-voter world would therefore
approximate the preferences of the median voter.[9]

Can we predict the outcome of the tax revolt in a median-voter world? In a strict sense, we could say very little unless we knew the exact range and distribution of preferences in each community or unless we assumed that they were identical. Cutting taxes in half would slice across different preference continua in different ways. But I do not think that we need to be that strict. The paucity of voter knowledge about the details of property taxes and referenda issues suggests that we can treat the vote on the Tisch amendment as a simple yes or no vote on the question of whether taxes are too high.[10] What can we say given this assumption? Tax-expenditure decisions based on median-voter preferences would be unsatisfactory to those with either above- or below-average demand for public goods. Only those with below-average demand would say that taxes are too high. Median voters are already satisfied while those with above-average demand would be even more dissatisfied if the level of public goods provision was moved still further from their preference position. A tax revolt could therefore occur but not succeed in a median-voter world. The median voters and those with above-average demand would form a majority opposed to the tax-revolt referenda. This pattern would not vary by jurisdictional characteristics as each jurisdiction would be at its own equilibrium level of public production leaving a sizable but interjurisdictionally constant minority in favor of a reduction in production relative to their own equilibrium point.

Revolt by the Majority: The Excessive-Government Model

Like the Tiebout model, the median-voter model has been criticized as unrealistic. As Deacon has written:

> The median-voter approach adopts a very simple view of seemingly complex political phenomena, and an apparent lack of realism has been a source of criticism. In particular, it neglects the activities of interest groups and assigns politicians the rather passive role of simply seeking out and supplying the demands of the voting middle class.[11]

The excessive-government model is based on this criticism. It posits a system where public goods are consistently overproduced or are perceived to be overproduced, and thus it has an obvious and direct relation to the tax revolt. Indeed, much of Howard Jarvis's rhetoric can be characterized as extremely rough popularization of this perspective.

The excessive-government model has two general strains. The first emphasizes the role of political and bureaucratic actors as strategic manipulators of fiscal institutions. The view of government as passive actor is rejected in favor of a view of politicians and bureaucrats as self-interested actors with a stake in the continued expansion of public production.[12] Given that self-interest, they establish fiscal institutions which obscure the true costs of public production and thereby increase the demand for public goods. The use of indirect taxes is commonly cited. As Buchanan and Wagner argue, "complex and indirect payment structures create a fiscal illusion that will systematically produce higher levels of public outlays than those that would be observed under simple payment structures."[13]

Beyond the general use of indirect taxes, several mechanisms designed to obscure the true level of property taxes have been observed. The first of these is underassessment, or the assessment of property at less than the legally required fraction of true cash value. Of course, the state equalization process corrects the artificially low assessments. But it is precisely that correction which enables the political and bureaucratic actors to benefit from underassessment. As John Shannon has written:

> The political implications of assessment reform are rather grim because for many state tax officials the decision to raise all local assessments to the state legal valuation standard places them in double jeopardy. First, local rate makers may take advantage of this situation by failing to cut back their tax rates commensurate with the state hike in local assessments. If this happens, then state officials will usually be blamed by irate property owners for the resultant increase in taxes.[14]

Equalization enables local government officials to avoid the public's wrath by shifting the perceived responsibility for higher taxes to the state. A second mechanism is differential assessment; those who can least influence the government's ability to garner votes are assessed at a higher-than-average fraction of true cash value. Local business property and the property of the poor are commonly overassessed.[15] They are relatively immobile, and in the case of the poor, relatively uninformed. This tax break to middle-income property owners lowers their perceived cost of public goods and thereby increases demand. Additionally, government can finance increased production through inflation increases in assessments. The rapid rise of housing values relative to the general price level has enabled government to increase property-tax revenue through increased assessment while claiming to be holding the line on taxes by maintaining a constant-tax rate. In Sherwood's words, "inflation takes the burden of decision off the legislators."[16] Once again, dissatisfaction is shifted away from local officials.

The evidence that such behavior occurs is persuasive. What remains unclear is whether the shifting of responsibility for higher taxes contributes to the tax revolt.[17] The excessive-government model suggests that it would. On inflation and underassessment, the breaking of the linkage between local electoral choices and local tax-expenditure decisions leaves the consumer-voter with little choice but to resort to extraordinary means to lower the level of public-goods production. Buchanan implied as much when he wrote: "attempts to reduce the excessive governmental spending might be aimed at the motivational structure of bureaucracy rather than at aggregate budgetary and tax levels. On the other hand, if the bureaucracy is considered to be so firmly entrenched and its institutions so rigid that direct attack would be futile, alternative means may be required."[18] Administrative improvements to reduce differential assessment may in fact start a tax revolt as middle-income consumer-voters are suddenly informed of the true costs of public production.[19] The first strain of the excessive-government model would lead us to expect greater support for tax-cutting referenda in jurisdictions with low-assessment levels (underassessment), rapid increases in housing prices, and recent reductions in differential assessment.

The second strain of the excessive-government model calls attention not to purposive behavior on the part of political and bureaucratic actors but to the technology of public production. Public goods may not be overproduced, but may be perceived to be overproduced because of the nature of public-production technology. Baumol argues that the large service component of public-goods production mandates rapidly rising expenditures.[20] This is so because productivity gains are much more difficult to secure in the service area.[21] Over time, the imbalance of productivity gains between the public and private sectors lead to a larger public sector. Expenditures and taxes will rise and will take a larger share of GNP with no change in the level of service.

Bradford, Malt, and Oates expanded on Baumol's work by suggesting that environmental factors may necessitate an increase in budgetary inputs in order to maintain a static level of public-goods production.[22] For example, the changing racial composition of cities has required increased spending to achieve the same level of performance.[23] Pettengill and Uppal concluded that, "The disadvantaged would require more educational dollars per pupil if they were to be raised to the national norm. . . . A high percentage of nonwhites in cities does raise educational costs."[24] General urban decline would have the same result; roads and schools must be maintained even if the tax base is declining or static.[25] In both cases, expenditures or taxes must go up to maintain a constant level of service because productivity gains cannot be relied on to make up the shortfall. As the consumer-voter sees rising taxes with no change in the level of service, one might expect him or her to view the government as excessive, wasteful, and inefficient. The second strain of the excessive-government model would lead us to expect greater support for tax-cutting referenda in jurisdictions characterized by changing racial compositon and general urban decline.

The excessive-government model, whether of the political/bureacratic or technological strain, would lead us to expect that on a general basis, governments with higher taxes would have a higher level of dissatisfaction with the production of public goods. We would expect to find greater support for tax-cutting proposals in these municipalities. While evidence supportive of this hypothesis has been found at the state level, exceptions are not inconceivable.[26] A low-tax government might have an even lower tax if there were no fiscal illusion. But the general relation seems plausible. This is particularly true given the political rhetoric surrounding the tax revolt.

Tax Crusade: The Interjurisdictional-Conflict Model

The models examined up to this point, including the Tiebout model, share the assumption that each community's decision on taxes and expenditures has no effect on any other community's decision. That assumption may be unwarranted given an understanding of the history of Michigan public finance. The vote on the Tisch amendment was not the first financial crisis in the state. In 1959, the state went bankrupt and had several payless pay-days due to a deadlock between the governor and legislature over new taxes.[27] Charles Press and Charles Adrian developed an explanation for that conflict that might be useful in explaining the more recent crisis.

Press and Adrian saw two very different public ideologies in the state. The first is the small-town ideology based on the rural past of Michigan. They noted that:

> The attitude toward government that followed from this belief system was, of course, that government should not spoil the process by interfering with it or by making wasteful expenditures that would deplete the capital of the entrepreneur. If government did little more than its traditional functions of keeping order and enforcing civil contract leaving other decisions in private hands, the land would flow with milk, honey, and the useful industrial artifacts of automobiles, zippers, and prepackaged breakfast foods.[28]

The other is the social-service state ideology of the cities which calls for a much broader role for public production.

If the two different types of communities dominated by these ideologies adopted local tax-expenditure decisions based on the median-voter model and left each other alone, there would be no problem. But Press and Adrian concluded that, "probably the most debilitating effect of the small-town ideology on state government today is the attempt to apply to all citizens the morality of small-town life of a half century ago."[29] They went on to explain the 1959 crisis as such an attempt by small-town legislators in a malapportioned senate to frustrate the urban majority represented by Governor Williams.

What would we expect to see if the same explanation is operative in the more recent crisis? First, we would expect the greatest support for the tax revolt to be found in the rural areas of the state. Press and Adrian suggest that the limited government ideology is rural-based. We could also examine the distribution of the two ideologies by identifying their impact on local public-production decisions. Jurisdictions dominated by the small-town ideology would have lower levels of production and taxes. Press and Adrian would lead us to expect that these units would attempt to impose their preferences on jurisdictions dominated by the social-service state ideology. We would expect, therefore, to find the greatest support for the tax revolt in the low-tax municipalities.

The three models are tested in the next section. Table 15–1 identifies the relationships with voter support for the tax revolt hypothesized by the three models. The critical variable is the level of taxation as the three models posit strikingly different relationships. The median-voter model suggests that the level of support would be constant and thus unrelated to the level of taxation. The excessive-government model would lead us to expect a positive relationship, while the interjurisdictional-conflict model hypothesizes that it will be negative.

Testing the Models

Data, Operationalization, and Estimation Procedures

An attempt was made to gather data on all 1,510 Michigan municipalities, but severe missing data problems were encountered so that data were gathered on only 696. To evaluate the representativeness of the sample, the sample and population values for five variables for which complete data

Table 15–1
Hypothesized Relationships of the Three Explanations of the Tax Revolt

	Median Voter	Excessive Government		Interjurisdictional Conflict
		Political-Bureaucratic/ Technological		
Level of taxation	0 [a]	+	+	−
Level of assessment	0	−	0	0
Reduction of differential assessment	0	+	0	0
Changing racial composition	0	0	+	0
Urban decline	0	0	+	0
Ruralness	0	0	0	+

[a] 0 = not statistically significant; + = positive and statistically significant; − = negative and statistically significant.

were available were compared. As seen in table 15-2, those five variables provide a broad description of Michigan municipalities on characteristics relevant to property taxation including the nature of the assessor's office, median income, median value of owner-occupied homes, the ratio of assessed to true cash or full market value, and population. The first was broken down into elected and appointed, while the others were trichotomized into values of high, medium, and low. As can be seen in comparing columns one and two of the table, the sample slightly overrepresents higher-income, better assessed, and more populous municipalities. The differences are small and should not seriously bias the results.[30]

The dependent variable is the level of support for the tax revolt. Michigan's 1978 election provides a unique opportunity to measure directly that support with the vote on the Tisch amendment. The level of support is therefore measured by the percentage of votes in favor of the Tisch amendment in each municipality (TD): a high value of TD represents a high level of support for the tax revolt.

The political/bureaucratic strain on the excessive-government model suggested three variables that would be related to the level of support for the tax revolt. Data were gathered on two.[31] The level of assessment is measured by the 1978 ratio of assessed value to full market value of all real property in a municipality (RATIO). Michigan law requires that all property be assessed at 50 percent of full market value; the lower RATIO is below 50 percent, the greater the degree of underassessment. This approach also suggested that any reduction in differential assessment may start a tax revolt as the full costs of public production are learned. Ideally, this should be measured by change in the dispersion of assessments. Unfortunately, the state of Michigan does not collect that information. Therefore, the difference between the 1978 and 1976 level of assessment (DIFF) is used as a proxy measure. Past research has indicated that the level and dispersion of assessments have a strong positive association.[32] A high value of DIFF indicates that there has been a reduction in differential assessment.

The technology strain of the excessive-government model calls attention to changes in the environment of public production. An increase in nonwhite population, for instance, may increase educational costs. This is measured by the percentage of population that is nonwhite (NWHITE). Unfortunately, this indicator is somewhat limited as it is static; it does not tap the rate of change. General urban decline was hypothesized to increase costs and therefore support for the tax revolt. Decline is measured by the percentage of year-round housing that is vacant for six months or more (VACANCY). A high percentage of vacancies indicates that a community has a static, if not declining, tax base. Additionally, a high-vacancy rate would depress housing prices and thus slow the growth of property-tax yield.

Table 15–2
Population and Sample Distributions on Community Characteristics

Community Characteristics	Sample N = 696	Population N = 1,510
Assessor's office		
Elected	56.8	57.0
Appointed	43.2	43.0
Median income		
Low	17.2	18.5
Medium	70.5	71.6
High	12.2	10.0
Median house value		
Low	32.0	33.6
Medium	34.1	36.2
High	33.9	30.1
Ratio of assessed to full market value		
Low	22.0	27.0
Medium	26.6	25.2
High	51.4	47.8
Population		
Low	68.2	74.0
Medium	15.8	14.6
High	15.9	11.5

The interjurisdictional-conflict model would lead us to expect high levels of support for the tax revolt in rural municipalities. Two measures are used to tap ruralness. The first is a dummy variable indicating whether a municipality is a city or a township (CITY). The seond is the percentage of property descriptions in the municipality used for agricultural or timber-cutover purposes (AGTIM).

The level of taxation is measured by the average combined municipal, county, and school district tax rate of each municipality (TAX). A full presentation of the definition, operationalization, and source of each variable can be seen in table 15–3.

A Goldfield-Quandt test indicated that the OLS estimates were heteroscedastic.[33] Several versions of a weighted least squares (WLS) procedure were undertaken to correct the estimates but so much multicollinearity was introduced with WLS that the results became uninterpretable. As a result, it was necessary to use the OLS estimates. They will be unbiased but not efficient so that caution should be exercised in interpreting the results; the significance levels will be somewhat deflated. There does not seem to be any severe multicollinearity problems as none of the R^2s produced by a Farrar-Glauber test exceed .6.[34]

Table 15-3
Definitions, Operationalizations, and Data Sources

Variable	Definition	Operationalization	Source
TD	Support for the tax revolt	Percent of affirmative votes for the Tisch Amendment, November 1978	Bureau of Elections: Michigan Secretary of State
RATIO	Level of assessment	1978 ratio of assessed value to full market value of real property	"1978 Factors, Assessed Valuation and Units. Portion of State Equalized Valuation" (Lansing, Mich.: State Tax Commission, 1978).
DIFF	Change in differential assessment	1978 ratio of assessed value to full market value minut 1976 ration of assessed value to full market value	"1978 Factors" and "1976 Factors, Assessed Valuation and Units. Portion of State Equalized Valuation" (Lansing, Mich.: State Tax Commission: 1976 & 1978).
NWHITE	Change in racial composition	Percent of population that is nonwhite	1970 U.S. census
VACANCY	Urban decline	Percent of year-round housing that is vacant for six months or more	1970 U.S. census
CITY	Ruralness #1	0, if township; 1, if city	"Directory of Assessors" (Lansing, Mich.: State Tax Commission, 1978).
AGTIM	Ruralness #2	Percent of property descriptions committed to agricultural or timber-cutover use	"Michigan Survey of Assessors and Equalization Directors" (Lansing, Mich.: Dept. of Treasury, 1976).
TAX	Level of taxation	1977 average combined tax rate	"1977 State Equalized Valuations and Average Tax Data" (Lansing, Mich.: State Tax Commission, 1976)

Findings

The regression results are presented in table 15-4. The results lend little support to the median-voter model. Contrary to the predictions of that model, three variables are strongly related to the level of support for the tax revolt: VACANCY, CITY, and TAX. (In light of the necessity to interpret the results conservatively because of the heteroskedasticity problem, it should be noted that all three have significance levels of less than .001.)

Table 15-4
Regression Results

Variable	Regression Coefficient	F Ratio	Standard Error	Significance Level
RATIO	− .058	1.937	.041	.164
DIFF	.048	.829	.053	.363
NWHITE	− .021	.212	.045	.646
VACANCY	.107	20.104	.024	.000
CITY	− 4.376	17.844	1.036	.000
AGTIM	− .014	.855	.015	.355
TAX	− .160	12.947	.044	.000
CONSTANT	53.133	368.884	2.766	.000

$R^2 = .203; R^2 = .195; F = 25.110; N = 696;$ significance levels $= .000$.

The excessive-government model fairs marginally better. The results provide only the slightest support for the first strain of that explanation. While the signs of the coefficients for DIFF and RATIO are in the predicted direction they are not significantly different from zero at the .05 level. The technological strain does somewhat better. The coefficient for NWHITE is neither in the predicted direction nor statistically significant. But VACANCY performs as predicted. The level of support for the tax revolt was higher in municipalities with high-vacancy rates.

The results lend somewhat greater support to the interjurisdictional-conflict model. Support for the tax revolt was much stronger in townships than in cities as indicated by the negative coefficient for CITY. The coefficient for AGTIM, however, was neither in the predicted direction nor statistically significant. More importantly, the highly significant negative relation between the level of taxation and support for the tax revolt is consistent with only the Press and Adrian explanation.

Conclusion

Two conclusions can be drawn from this preliminary effort to develop a theory of the tax revolt. First, analysis of the three alternative models tells us very little about the tax revolt in a positive sense. Most of the variance in support for the tax revolt remains unexplained. This essentially negative conclusion is important, however, as the median-voter and excessive-government models are the two dominant approaches used in explaining public-sector production. The results cast some doubt on their utility in explaining the tax revolt (at least in their most simplified forms as presented here).

Second, the interjurisdictional-conflict model results suggest another approach to explaining the tax revolt. The TAX and CITY findings lend some support to that explanation. Obviously, the results are hardly definitive. Much of the variance is not accounted for. More importantly, this alternative model is only weakly developed. Press and Adrian were concerned with broad historical interpretation rather than working out a detailed model of the processes of interjurisdictional interaction in production decisions. But the findings do suggest that greater attention be directed to social-psychological characteristics and decision externalities in developing an explanation of the tax revolt; factors that are explicitly excluded from the other two models.[35] Effort should be directed at refining the interjurisdictional-conflict model including the processes through which local ideology is interjurisdictionally exercised in policy disputes.

These conclusions must be tempered by several limitations in this analysis. First, improvement in the operationalization of the three models is needed. Only a very limited set of the political and bureaucratic strategies associated with the excessive-government model was considered. Racial composition and vacancy rates hardly exhaust the range of environmental factors affecting public production. And the use of the proxy measures DIFF and NWHITE could certainly be improved upon. Second, the generalizability of the results is questionable. I have tried to explain the tax revolt when in fact there may be many tax revolts. The interjurisdictional-conflict model fits Michigan's public finance history but may not be applicable elsewhere. Certainly, the rapid rise of housing prices in California coupled with reductions in differential assessment following the 1967 assessment reforms suggests that the excessive-government explanation may be more important in that state.[36] No single explanation will do if there are many different kinds of tax revolts. Whether there is one tax revolt or many is a research question that is as yet unanswered.

Finally, what can we say about the tax revolt if the Tiebout model is used as a standard for judging institutional change in the provision of public goods? To the extent that we can characterize the tax revolt as a crusade by low-tax jurisdictions to impose their preferences on high-tax jurisdictions, the revolt clearly represents a departure from a Tiebout-like world. A successful tax revolt would move consumer-voters even further away from the optimal level of public goods provision as their range of choice is restricted. This is ironic in that the Tiebout standard is more commonly used to criticize the imposition of high-tax preferences on low-tax jurisdictions through metropolitanization.[37] Interjurisdictional imperialism may not be restricted to the big spenders.

Notes

1. Jerry McCaffery and John H. Bowman, "Participatory Democracy and Budgeting: The Effects of Proposition 13," *Public Administration Review* 38 (November/December 1978):530–538.

2. Selma J. Mushkin, *Proposition 13 and Its Consequences for Public Management* (Cambridge, Mass.: Abt Books, 1974); Jack Citrin, "Do People Want Something for Nothing: Public Opinion on Taxes and Government Spending," *National Tax Journal Supplement* 32 (June 1979): 113–119; Richard Attiyeh and Robert F. Engle, "Testing Some Propositions about Proposition 13," *National Tax Journal* 32 (June 1979): 131–146.

3. This literature cited examines voter expectations about the results of tax limitation: would services be severely cut or only "bureaucratic fat" trimmed? Answering this question indirectly relates to the issue of explaining the tax revolt. If voters intended and expected services to be drastically cut, one might infer that the excessive-government model accounts for the overproduction of public goods. There are a number of problems with this literature, however. First, the issue of voter expectations examined in this literature is treated rather narrowly. This research is primarily descriptive with only limited effort given to the broader issues implicit in the models presented here. Second, the results are highly ambiguous. Working with similar data, Attiyeh and Engle reach a conclusion that is the polar opposite of those of Mushkin and Citrin. This type of research is important as suggested in my conclusion. But its utility will be increased if it is related to a broader theoretical understanding of tax revolt which is the subject addressed here.

4. Steve Mariotti, "An Economic Analysis of the Voting on Michigan's Tax and Expenditure Limitation Amendment," *Public Choice* 33, no. 3 (1978):15–26; Paul N. Courant, Edward M. Gramlich, and Daniel Rubinfeld, "Tax Limitation and the Demand for Public Services in Michigan," *National Tax Journal* 32 (June 1979):147–158.

5. Very interestingly, both of these articles use Michigan data. They are quite different from the present effort, however. Most importantly, both restrict themselves to examining a single model of the tax revolt rather than testing alternative models against each other. Mariotti, moreover, examined Michigan's vote on Proposal C in 1976. Proposal C dealt with state-level tax limitation by relating state taxes to personal income. This is very different from the 1978 vote on the Tisch amendment which would have slashed local property taxes. He also limited himself to the narrower issue of whether voting was based on economic self-interest and his results were inconclusive. Courant, Gramlich, and Rubinfeld did examine the Tisch vote. The article cited here presents a model based on public employee

voting. It did not present, however, the results of the test which have yet to be published.

6. Charles M. Tiebout, "A Pure Theory of Local Expenditures," *Journal of Political Economy* 44 (October 1956):418.

7. My parentheses.

8. Howard Pack and Janet R. Pack, "Metropolitan Fragmentation and Local Public Expenditures," *National Tax Journal* 31 (December 1978):359.

9. James M. Buchanan and Gordon Tullock, *The Calculus of Consent* (Ann Arbor, Mich.: University of Michigan Press, 1962), pp. 131–145; James L. Barr and Otto A. Davis, "An Elementary Political and Economic Theory of the Expenditures of Local Governments," *Southern Economic Journal* 33 (October 1966):413–426; William A. McEachern, "Collective Decision Rules and Local Debt Choice: A Test of the Median-Voter Hypothesis," *National Tax Journal* 31 (June 1978):129–136.

10. Most property-tax analysts conclude that taxpayers are very uninformed about how the property tax works. Unless consumer-voters are informed on how the tax works, precise calculations of how referenda choice relate to their preferences would be difficult if not impossible. Treating the tax revolt as a yes or no vote on the question of whether taxes are too high merely recognizes that consumer-voters are uninformed on this issue. This initial uncertainty about property taxes is confounded further by the campaigns on tax-limitation proposals. Lack of information and deliberate misinformation leave voters very uncertain in making tax-limitation choices. Voting on the question of whether taxes are too high would seem to be a plausible strategy under these circumstances. For a discussion of the use of information and misinformation in tax-revolt campaigns, see Mariotti, "Michigan's Limitation Amendment, p. 25.

11. Robert T. Deacon, "Private Choice and Collective Outcomes: Evidence from Public Sector Demand Analysis." *National Tax Journal* 30 (December 1977):379; also see Helen F. Ladd, "An Economic Evaluation of State Limitation on Local Taxing and Spending Powers," *National Tax Journal* 31 (March 1978):4.

12. Anthony Downs, *Inside Bureaucracy* (Boston: Little, Brown and Co., 1967); William A. Niskanan, *Bureaucracy and Representative Government* (Chicago: Aldine and Atherton, 1971); Thomas E. Borcherding, ed., *Budgets and Bureaucrats: The Sources of Government Growth* (Durham, N.C.: Duke University Press, 1977).

13. James M. Buchanan and Richard E. Wagner, *Democracy in Deficit: The Political Legacy of Lord Keynes* (New York: Academic Press, 1977), p. 129.

14. John Shannon, "The Property Tax: Reform or Relief?" in

Property Tax Reform, ed. George E. Peterson (Washington, D.C.: Urban Institute, 1973), p. 32.

15. Henry Aaron and Oliver Oldman, "Assessment-Sales Ratios under the Boston Property Tax," *National Tax Journal* 18 (March 1965):153–156; Diane Paul, *The Politics of the Property Tax* (Lexington, Mass.: Lexington Books, D.C. Heath and Co., 1975).

16. Frank Sherwood, "Inflation Fuels Proposition 13," *Public Administration Times* (July 1978):12.

17. The literature on fiscal illusion provides no clear answer. For contrasting views on the effect of fiscal illusion on expenditures, see David R. Cameron, "The Expansion of the Public Economy: A Comparative Analysis," *American Political Science Review* 72 (December 1978): 1243–1261, and Charles J. Goetz, "Fiscal Illusion in State and Local Finance," in Borcherding, *Budgets and Bureaucrats,* pp. 176–187.

18. James M. Buchanan, "Why Does Government Grow?" in Borcherding, *Budgets and Bureaucrats,* p. 5.

19. Shannon, "Property Tax," p. 32.

20. Neoclassical public-choice analysts would argue that it is not technology per se but the noncompetitive nature of the public sector that inhibits productivity gains. While acceptance of this alternative explanation would change the type of corrective policy one would look at, it does not alter the more general hypotheses developed here. For an exposition of the neoclassical view, see Robert M. Spann, "Public versus Private Provision of Governmental Services," in Borcherding, *Budgets and Bureaucrats,* pp. 100–129.

21. William J. Baumol, "Macroeconomics of Unbalanced Growth: The Anatomy of Urban Crisis," *American Economic Review*" 57 (June 1967):415–426.

22. D.F. Bradford; R.A. Malt; and W.E. Oates, "The Rising Costs of Local Public Services: Some Evidence and Reflections," *National Tax Journal* 22 (June 1969):185–201.

23. Werner Z. Hirsch et al., *Fiscal Pressures on the Central City* (New York: Praeger, 1971), p. 5.

24. Robert B. Pettengill and Jogindar Uppal, *Can the Cities Survive? The Fiscal Plight of American Cities* (New York: St. Martin Press, 1974), p. 20.

25. Arnold Meltsner, *The Politics of City Revenue* (Berkeley, Calif.: University of California Press, 1971), p. 17.

26. Ladd, "Economic Limitation," p. 2.

27. Carolyn Stieber, *The Politics of Change in Michigan* (East Lansing, Mich.: Michigan State University Press, 1970), pp. 9–14.

28. Charles Press and Charles R. Adrian, "Why Our State Govern-

ments Are Sick?" *The Grass Roots,* ed., Edwin C. Buell and William E. Brigman (Glenview, Ill.: Scott, Foresman and Co., 1968), p. 15.

29. Ibid., p. 19.

30. The sample was weighted to match to population values on these five variables in a separate analysis. The regression results of the weighted sample were only slightly different from those for the unweighted sample presented here.

31. Jurisdictional-level data on inflation in housing prices were not available.

32. James A. Maxwell, *Financing State and Local Governments* (Washington, D.C.: Brookings Institution, 1969), pp. 137–142; John H. Bowman and John L. Mikesell, "Uniform Assessment of Property: Returns from Institutional Remedies," *National Tax Journal* 31 (June 1978):137–152.

33. The Goldfield-Quandt test produced an F of 1.66 where the critical value of F is 1.00 at the .05 level. For a discussion of the G-Q test, see Robert S. Pindyck and Daniel Rubinfeld, *Econometric Models and Economic Forecasts* (New York: McGraw-Hill Book Co., 1976), pp. 104–106.

34. The Farrar-Glauber test R^2 are as follows for each of the independent variables: NWHITE (.02), VACANCY (.14), DIFF (.24), CITY (.58), AGTIM (.32), TAX (.58), and RATIO (.25). For a discussion of the F-G test, see Jan Kmenta, *Elements of Econometrics* (New York: Mcmillan Publishing Co., 1971), p. 390.

35. Mariotti's failure to consider noneconomic factors as suggested here may account for his very inconclusive results. Tax-referenda voting may not be dependent on self-interest as narrowly defined in both the median-voter and excessive-government models. The development of an alternative model which broadens the factors considered in determining voter self-interest would seem to be necessary to explain the tax-revolt voting.

36. Paul, *Property Tax,* p. 97.

37. Robert L. Bish, *The Public Economy of Metropolitan Areas* (Chicago: Markham, 1971); Robert L. Bish and Vincent Ostrom, *Understanding Urban Government* (Washington, D.C.: American Enterprise Institute, 1973); Vincent Ostrom, *The Intellectual Crisis in American Public Administration* (University, Ala.: University of Alabama Press, 1974).

16 Interregional Benefits from Federal Spending: A New Look at an Old Issue

William F. Fox and
J. Norman Reid

Introduction

Since 1968 the federal government has compiled annually a comprehensive report on spending by its executive branch agencies (U.S. Community Services Administration). These reports—known popularly as the federal outlays—provide a detailed source of data on spending under more than 1,500 federal programs in the nation's counties and in cities over 25,000 population. The comprehensiveness and detail of the data offer excellent opportunities for evaluating federal spending policies. These are restricted somewhat, however, by several shortcomings of the data (Reid 1978; Anton 1979). Chief among these is the fact that large proportions of the county- and city-level detail are estimated. While some of these estimation methods appear to be valid, others are clearly unacceptable, making it necessary to analyze federal programs selectively. Further problems arise from the rather sketchy documentation available on the individual programs included in the reports.

Despite these problems, a number of recent studies have used the federal outlays data to analyze the distribution of federal expenditures. The issue attracting the most interest has been the interregional flow of funds (Havemann, Stanfield, and Peirce 1976). Other studies, however, have made full use of the geographic detail in the outlays data to examine trends below the state level. Some of these have assessed federal aid to cities (Dye and Hurley 1978; Anton 1979), while others have measured the distribution of spending between urban and rural areas (Reid, Godsey, and Hines 1978) or among areas with varying levels of economic development (U.S. Congressional Budget Office 1977).

These studies are similar in assuming that the benefits from the spending are proportional to each area's share of total outlays. Even though the mix of programs, as well as their probable impact, varies from place to place, most attention has centered on the first round distribution of dollars and little study has been given to tracing subsequent shifts or measuring ultimate impacts.

149

Economic Effects of Federal Outlays

An area's share of federal spending is usually a misleading surrogate for the economic effects which result from that funding. Several kinds of economic effects can be expected to result, including increased employment, income creation, and unemployment reduction. Depending on the way in which the dollars come into the area, as well as some characteristics of the geographic area itself discussed below, very different economic effects can result from a given expenditure.

The multiplier concept has been developed as a way to summarize the economic effects, whether income or employment, of a given stimulus.[1] The income multiplier is defined as the amount by which a one-dollar income stimulus, such as an outlay, increases community income. For example, a multiplier of 1.5 means that a federal outlay of $10,000 eventually leads to a $15,000 total increase in community income.

Some portion of federal expenditure immediately becomes local income. In addition, use of this direct income stimulus to purchase goods and services from local merchants causes an indirect income increase. The process is continued so long as merchants and workers spend and respend these monies within the community. Through successive cycles of spending for locally provided goods and services, the multiplier process is created.

Unfortunately no single multiplier exists. Multipliers vary according to the size and composition of the geographic area to which the multiplier is being applied. The multiplier concept can be used for areas ranging in size from individual communities to the nation as a whole, though for comparisons of economic stimulation, the smaller geographic areas, such as communities or states, are generally used. A general principle is that the smaller and less diverse the areas being analyzed, the smaller the multiplier will be. The following discussion deals with community multipliers.

The multiplier appropriate for examining economic effects differs across communities and for different types of stimuli within a community. The important determinants of the multiplier are the proportion of each outlay dollar which is added directly to residents' income and the propensity to spend and respend that income within the community. The size of the direct addition to community income depends on the extent to which the income recipients (for example, laborers) actually reside in the community, the proportion of the federal dollars which are used to buy goods rather than labor, and the degree to which the income replaces rather than adds to other income sources. Larger amounts of spending added directly to resident incomes mean a higher multiplier and therefore a greater economic stimulus.

The multiplier is also affected by the extent to which the income is saved, used to pay off existing debts, or used to purchase goods produced outside the community. A higher propensity to spend the income and to spend it in such a way that it will be respent within the same community means a larger multiplier and a greater economic stimulus to the area.

Federal income transfers to individuals make the largest direct contributions to community income, because the initial federal dollars are totally added to resident income. As a result, the income multipliers for these programs are likely to be the largest of any federal activity.

Federal purchases of goods and services will probably have a lower effect on income because larger portions of the expenditure will go for items at least part of which will be produced outside the community. However, there should be some differences in the multiplier effect depending on what is purchased. Local income should receive a larger increase from the purchase of those goods and services with large labor components because a greater share of the expenditure is likely to be kept in the community as local salaries. Construction activities, for example, are likely to have higher local labor components than many types of manufacturing, so the multipliers will be larger. Thus, income transfers are likely to have the greatest economic effect, followed by spending for construction (or other labor-intensive activities), and finally, purchases of more capital-intensive or assembly-oriented goods.

A final consideration is the way in which the funds are provided. Federal grants and direct payments are provided with no explicit return to the federal coffers anticipated. Loan funds, on the other hand, provide an economic stimulation when given, but presumably cause a reduction in local economic activity at some future time as the funds are paid back. The net increase to the community may only be the subsidized interest cost of money. Loan guarantees may represent a similar circumstance. However, unlike direct loans, guaranteed loans are not financed by the federal treasury and except in case of default, the net economic effect may only be a subsidized interest cost as lenders see a lower risk associated with a loan. Thus, we expect grants or direct payments to provide the greatest economic stimulation, followed by loans and then loan guarantees.

Actual estimation of multipliers must be done separately for each individual geographic area and for each economic sector. Input-output coefficients or regional-economic models are particularly useful for estimating the size of multipliers. Although not done for individual economic sectors, a recent study estimated regional and state multipliers for federal grants-in-aid payments (Gustely and Ballard 1979).[2] The average national multiplier was 2.0, with multipliers varying widely by states and by region. Further, the total stimulative effect did not occur for seven years, though two-thirds of the effect did occur in the first year. Colorado was found to be the lowest state, with a multiplier of 0.7; Michigan was highest, with 3.3. Because of the greater possibilities for leakage, community-level multipliers are lower than those for larger areas such as states, and in all likelihood range between 1.0 and 2.0 (generally nearer to 1.0) for most economic sectors and stimuli.

The data presented below are for regions of the nation rather than for smaller geographic areas. This is done to highlight the sector and financing differences in federal outlays, though the variations within regions suggest that more disaggregated data would also be informative.

Findings

Federal outlays, as reported by the Community Services Administration, totaled $499.5 billion in fiscal 1978. Of this total, some $457.8 billion can be tracked to the regional level; these were divided among analytic categories based on the amount of local labor each program buys and the type of federal program involved.

Income programs include such diverse activities as federal salaries, retirement benefits, and public assistance. Highway and dam building are examples of construction programs. Manufacturing outlays subsume military hardware, supplies, and many other purchases. The percentage of each region's per capita outlays derived from each type of program is given in table 16-1.

It is not possible to estimate the total economic impact of federal programs without estimating program multipliers, an effort which would be massive indeed and beyond our scope here. However, comparing the level and percentage of regional outlays allocated under each type of program gives an indication of likely differences in the economic impact of these outlays in communities within each region.

Per capita total outlays were highest in the West, followed closely by the South. They were lowest in the North Central states where average per capita outlays were 83 percent of the level for the United States as a whole. These findings are consistent with the trends reported by numerous observers during recent years.

In addition to grants-in-aid and other expenditures, the totals include new commitments of direct loans and the amounts of private-sector loans guaranteed under federal housing and other programs during fiscal 1978. Loans per capita are highest in the West and South and lowest in the Northeast; when only per capita expenditures (direct spending and grants) are compared, the differences among the regions are narrower than for total outlays; the ordering of the regions remains unchanged, however.

In general, the West and South also have the highest per capita outlays for each program category. Outlays resulting directly in income account for just under two-thirds of the total. Per capita outlays for these programs are

Table 16-1
Federal Outlays by Program Category and Census Region, Fiscal Year 1978

	1	2	3	4	5
Expenditure Object and Census Region	*Total*	*Direct Federal Spending*	*Grants*	*Direct Loans*	*Guaranteed Loans*
Percent of regional outlays					
Income					
Northeast	66.7	90.4[a]	8.8	0.0	0.7
North Central	69.3	84.6[a]	7.6	5.3	2.5
South	66.5	88.9[a]	7.2	1.6	2.3
West	59.1	89.3[a]	8.1	1.2	1.4
United States	65.6	88.3[a]	7.8	2.1	1.8
Construction					
Northeast	8.5	41.2	12.9	1.2	44.7
North Central	14.4	36.1	4.9	0.7	58.3
South	14.4	36.8	4.9	0.0	58.3
West	16.5	31.8	3.6	0.7	63.9
United States	13.6	35.5	5.8	0.7	58.1
Manufactured goods					
Northeast	24.7	81.8	12.1	2.0	4.0
North Central	16.3	78.6	11.3	3.8	6.2
South	19.1	78.8	11.0	4.8	5.3
West	24.4	88.7	6.2	1.6	3.4
United States	20.8	81.7	10.1	3.4	4.8
Per capita outlays					
Total					
Northeast	$1910	$1605[a]	$191	$13	$102
North Central	1750	1340[a]	136	77	196
South	2325	1846[a]	178	47	255
West	2544	2027[a]	176	32	309
United States	2116	1688[a]	169	45	214

Source: U.S. Community Services Administration, *Distribution of Federal Funds,* Fiscal 1978.

Note: Numbers in column 1 represent percentages of regional total. Numbers in columns 2, 3, 4, and 5 represent percentage of column 1.

[a] Includes grants for major income transfer programs providing direct benefits to recipients.

slightly higher in the South ($1,547) than the West ($1,504), but each is considerably higher than in the Northeast ($1,275) and North Central ($1,213) regions. A similar relationship occurs when only expenditure programs are compared, except that the North Central region is relatively worse off due to the high levels of per capita farm loans it receives ($93).

Nationally, outlays for programs in which construction is a major product amount to some 14 percent of the total, or $288 per capita. These are highest in the West, where they amount to 145 percent of the U.S. average per capita, followed by the South ($334) and North Central region

($252). This category is dominated by housing loan programs, which make up over half the total. When only grants and other spending are compared, the advantage of the sunbelt is reduced, though not eliminated.

The final category of programs—those which result in major purchases of manufactured goods—account for 21 percent of the total, or $439 per capita nationally. Outlays for these programs, both in total and for spending programs alone, are highest in the West and second highest in the industrial Northeast; they are lowest in the North Central region. Little difference in the relative distributions can be observed when only expenditures are considered.

Despite its overall low level of outlays, total outlays in the North Central region include a higher proportion of income programs (69 percent), as well as a lower proportion of manufactured goods programs (16 percent), than any other region, giving this region the most beneficial mix of programs. The South and the Northeast each received two-thirds of their total outlays for income programs, though the South receives more of the remainder for construction programs than the Northeast, where a larger share of outlays go for manufactured goods. The mix of programs is least beneficial in the West, where only 59 percent goes for income, while the proportions for construction and manufactured goods are higher than any other region. When the loan programs are removed, these same regional differences are even more pronounced, due mainly to the importance of loan programs as a part of total outlays in the North Central region.

Conclusion

This research sheds new light on the already much studied issue of the inter-regional distribution of federal funds. It suggests that overall regional trends in per capita outlays may not reflect accurately the distribution of economic benefits. Outlays in the North Central region include the highest percentage of income programs—programs with the highest expected community multipliers—while the mix of outlays in the West includes the lowest proportion of income programs, and so is subject to the lowest multiplier effect per dollar of outlays. This pattern is directly opposite to the pattern for regional per capita outlays and it underscores the importance of looking beyond the aggregate distribution of initial federal payments.

In addition, these data demonstrate the importance of paying attention to different types of programs, since it clearly matters whether a community's outlays are made up of direct spending or of loaned monies. Loans are much more significant to the North Central states than to any other region—due mainly to the larger amounts of farm loans made in the region—and when only federal spending (and not total federal outlays) in the regions is examined, the apparent relative disadvantage to the North Central states is exacerbated.

These findings also have important implications for the success of federal efforts to redistribute income among the regions. The South, which has the lowest overall per capita income levels and has been the special target of economic development programs, shares a double benefit from federal spending. Not only does it rank high in per capita outlays (only slightly lower than the West), but its total also includes a relatively beneficial mix of programs, second only to the North Central region in the percentage comprised of income programs. On the basis of this evidence, it seems probable that the highest total economic benefits from federal funds accrue to the South and that federal redistributive policies are thus at least moderately successful when measured on a regional basis.

Notes

1. Employment multipliers are not discussed here.

2. This study estimated gross state output multipliers rather than income multipliers.

References

Anton, Thomas J. "Outlays Data and the Analysis of Federal Policy Data." Paper presented at the Urban Impacts of Federal Policies Conference, Washington, D.C., 8–9 February 1979.

Dye, Thomas R., and Thomas L. Hurley. "The Responsiveness of Federal and State Governments to Urban Problems." *Journal of Politics* 40 (February 1978): 196–207.

Gustely, Richard D., and Kenneth P. Ballard. "Federal Grants and Regional Growth: An Analysis of Policy Impacts." Paper presented at the Southern Economic Association Conference, Atlanta, Georgia, 7–9 November 1979.

Havemann, Joel, Rochelle L. Stanfield, and Neal R. Peirce. "Federal Spending: The North's Loss Is the Sunbelt's Gain." *National Journal* 8 (26 June 1976): 878–891.

Reid, J. Norman. "Understanding Federal Program: The Need for a Coordinated Data System." *State and Local Government Review* (May 1979): 42–47.

Reid, J. Norman, W. Maureen Godsey, and Fred K. Hines. *Federal Outlays in Fiscal 1976: A Comparison of Metropolitan and Nonmetropolitan Areas.* Rural Development Research Report No. 1 (Washington: Economics, Statistics, and Cooperatives Services, U.S. Department of Agriculture, August 1978.

U.S. Community Services Administration. *Geographic Distribution of Federal Funds.* Springfield, Va.: National Technical Information Service, annual.

U.S. Congressional Budget Office. *Troubled Local Economies and the Distribution of Federal Dollars.* Washington: U.S. Government Printing Office, August 1977.

Part VI
Theoretical Perspectives

17

Interdependence and Impacts: Toward the Integration of Externality, Public Goods, and Grants Theories

Warren J. Samuels and
A. Allan Schmid

From at least the middle decades of the eighteenth century to the present a fundamental insight, even theorem, of economics has been the general interconnectedness of all economic variables. The conduct of most economic analysis has tended, however, to focus on the choices made by essentially autonomous individuals from within their respective opportunity sets (the sets of alternatives open to each of them). Lurking in the background has been the recognition of the general interconnectedness of all variables and, by inference, the general interdependence of economic actors and their opportunity sets. (Interdependence has been recognized as making economic analysis exceedingly intractable. Partial equilibrium solutions often have been allowed to serve as proxies for less-determinate general equilibrium solutions.) Until relatively late in the twentieth century, economists did not have a body of theory (except insofar as the general theory of the market per se may be so described) which dealt explicitly and systematically with interdependence and even then it has been considered and treated as the incidental exception to the general analysis of voluntary exchange self-contained among autonomous actors in the market.

Actually, three bodies of theory have been developed which attempt to explore and capture the nuances—and particularly implications for government policy, especially public expenditure—of interdependence: the theories of externalities, public goods, and grants. They have provided three sets of heterogeneous handles on or conceptualizations of a common problem or feature of economic activity: interdependence and the impacts on individual opportunity sets produced thereby. However, these bodies of theory, particularly externality and public goods, have defined their problems relatively narrowly and have tended to utilize models of voluntary exchange by autonomous individuals, thereby failing to capture the diverse breadth and depth of interdependence.

The purpose here is to present a preliminary analysis which is more general than any one of the three theories alone. The analysis explicitly and directly, albeit schematically, explores impacts as a function of interdependence and is intended to identify the problem of integrating the three into a more coherent, more complete, and also less normatively presumptive approach, and to develop some fundamentals concerning the area of analysis formed by the three theories. The first part examines various facets of the conventional treatment. The second part identifies the elements of the opportunity-set model used here as an approach to general interdependence. Part three examines impacts: their general nature, the conditions which govern their genesis, and a tentative taxonomy of impact situations.

The Extant Theories

Several points should be made with regard to the three existing bodies of theory. First, externality and public-goods theories have developed within mainstream economics and have come to form a large part of public-expenditure theory notwithstanding their diverse origins and the heterogeneous content of each. Grants theory is the most recent development and has been less if at all integrated into mainstream public-expenditure theory. Second, most work in all three areas has been taxonomic and definitional. Third, much work has been directed at producing statements of the formal, technical (necessary) conditions of determinate, optimal solutions.

Fourth, especially in the areas of externality and public-goods theories, there have been heterogeneous and conflicting sets of models (for example, varieties of perfect and mixed public goods) each existing in an ambiguous relation to the others, the operative fundamental conception (of externality or of public goods, and of their relation to each other, when discussed) perceived differently in different models and contexts. Accordingly, the three bodies of theory, considered separately or together, provide three ambiguously related sets of heterogeneous handles on interdependence.

Fifth, much attention has focused on the economic nature of goods, in many cases on fundamental characteristics of their production, cost sharing, supply, or consumption serving as definitional criteria (for example, pecuniary versus technological externalities, joint supply, nonexclusion) applied to classifications of types of goods or the nature of the exchange or other mode of transmission as well as the nature of "publicness." Sixth, in part because of the general disciplinary preoccupation with markets per se (and the optimality features of voluntary exchange therein), much attention has focused on the nature and extent of market failures. Seventh, externality and public-goods theories frequently have been conjoined with some form of benefit-cost analysis, involving the prefiguring specification of costs and benefits.

Eighth, some attention, within various applications of voluntary-exchange models and sundry specifications of public-choice models, has been given to reaching conclusions as to underproduction (supply) versus overproduction (supply) of public goods and externalities. Ninth, considerable effort has been expended to reach normative (as distinct from formal) conclusions as to externality and public-goods policy, whether achieved privately, governmentally, or in some combination. There has been considerable concern given to formulating solutions to perceived problems or to opportunities for governmental corrective action (of various types). There also has been considerable concern with the critique and defense of laissez faire and market solutions, even to the extent of embattling the conventional productivity principle of distribution.

Tenth, insofar as utility analysis has been used, individual (as contrasted with planners) preferences have been relied upon. Eleventh, a vast array of inevitably complicating considerations has entered discussion and analysis, for example, the relation of individual consumption to total supply and to other consumers, optional vis-à-vis nonoptional exposure, differential conditions of access and exposure, availability as compared with utilization, local vis-à-vis national public goods, and free in relation to forced riders.

Twelfth, conventional usages have selectively narrowed analytic treatment and thereby presumptively channeled the application of theory to policy. Four examples may be given. First, varying differentiations of public from private goods have respectively narrowed or broadened the scope of corrective expenditure or regulatory policy by government (but typically without specific conclusive application to particular issues of policy). Second, the distinction between (merely) pecuniary externalities, which are transmitted through price and quantity changes within the market (and therefore not true externalities), and technological externalities, which, in addition to being thought to escape market price and quantity determination, are perceived as affecting production-technological opportunities, artificially and presumptively excludes from consideration vast ranges of interdependence. Third, implicit in the distinction between pecuniary and technological externalities but also existing independently, is the notion that (true) externalities are not internalized by an economic actor and especially not captured by the market. This too is artificially narrowing: the costs of pollution, for example, are felt by (indeed, internalized by) pollutees, affecting their costs, purchases, prices, and so on, all within the markets for their input and output if not the markets for the polluter's input and product. Fourth, the distinction between Pareto-relevant and Pareto-irrelevant externalities, based upon whether or not internalizing trades are generated, while underscoring the possibilities or promoting private solutions, encounters (in both large and small number cases, in varying degrees) problems of transaction costs, free and forced riders, and strategic behavior— each involving further aspects of interdependence, and moreover selectively narrowing the ostensible field for externality analysis and policy.

The following analysis shares several of those characteristics. It is taxonomic and broadening rather than artificially narrowing. It is neutral with regard to policy rather than presumptively channeling. It is not directed to the production of either determinate or optimal solutions. It focuses on the nature of the interrelationships constituting interdependence and productive of impacts, and not solely on the nature or sources of goods as a basis of those interrelations. It is concerned with interdependence per se, not with market success or failure. Above all, it is concerned with all impacts and with integrating the variegated insights of externality, public goods, and grants theories. In the case of externality theory, the insights have come about through the various modelings of externality (say, by Pigovians and Paretians). In the case of public goods theory (which is largely but not exclusively Paretian), they have been realized through the construction of definitions and taxonomies utilizing the two major criteria of nonexclusion (and costly exclusion) and joint supply as well as supplemental (and sometimes principal) criteria such as nonappropriability, individual nonadjustment of quantity, transaction costs, indivisibilities, and increasing returns. In the case of grants theory, insights have been achieved through such taxonomies and analyses as gift versus tribute, explicit versus implicit grants, positive and negative grants, grantor versus grantee determination, voluntary versus involuntary, and optional versus nonoptional.

If one thinks about it, externalities, public goods, and grants unquestionably have much in common and appear to probe the same range of worldly phenomena. Externalities deal with costs and benefits visited upon parties other than the acting or contracting ones. Given the reciprocal character of externalities, the parties are in a situation in which one party or the other will be impacted either by the action of the other party or by governmental corrective policy. The question is not whether there will be an externality, but which externality will be permitted, its reciprocal being inhibited. Public-goods situations tend to involve impacts upon other parties through the provision of goods to or by one party which ipso facto are supplied to the other at no additional cost of production but with costly exclusion or avoidance if indeed any is physically possible. Grants involve unilateral transfers which, whatever their respective preference functions, impact upon the net worth and opportunity-set positions of grantor and grantee. Externality and public goods situations seem clearly to involve grants of one kind or another to second or third parties, grants which may or may not be welcome, and which have impact on respective opportunity sets. All three bodies of theory deal with models of the generation or transmission and receipt of impacts of the actions, voluntary or involuntary, of other acting parties.

That there are relations, for example, certain overlapping between externalities and public goods, is commonplace and an a priori justification for efforts to systematize if not to integrate the two respective bodies of theory. Thus, one finds in the literature lines of reasoning which attempt to differentiate externalities from public goods as well as others which attempt to equate them; which ignore or emphasize, respectively, the public good aspect of externalities or the externality aspect of public goods; which stress that externalities are a subcategory of public goods (say, emphasizing joint-ness of supply) or that public goods are a subcategory of externalities; which stress that externalities and jointness of supply are intrinsic to a(nother) concept of collective goods; and which indicate the possibility of activity providing both collective or public goods and externalities simul-taneously (in each case a function of the particular definition used). That there are relations between externality and public-goods theories and grants theory is indicated by recalling lines of reasoning which identify the grant (unilateral transfer) element (positive or negative) in externalities and public goods and the externality or public-goods aspects of grants. Moreover, cer-tain complicating considerations enter all three bodies of theory, such as optional versus nonoptional, voluntary versus nonvoluntary, differential conditions of access and of exposure, availability versus utilization, and even explicit versus implicit. The apparent commonalities of the three bodies of theory, the fact that each represents an attempt to comprehend interdependence, and the importance of both the theoretical and policy issues involved therein, seems to warrant effort to integrate the three or to collapse them in a more general analysis, however much any particular inte-gration may fail to capture the richness of each body of theory and there-fore be less than all-encompassing.

Interdependence: The Opportunity-Set Model

The economy is a complex decision-making process. Economic actors parti-cipate through making choices from within their respective opportunity sets. At any point in time there is a structure of opportunity sets (represent-ing the distribution of disaggregated opportunity) and of the underlying power on which in part opportunity sets are based. Through time there is a complex network of paths followed by individual opportunity sets and of the underlying power relationships on which they are in part based.

Interdependence arises in that decisions by individual economic actors or subgroups, either qua individuals or through the aggregation of individ-ual decisions, have impact on the opportunity sets of other actors or sub-groups. Economic reality permits at least two quite disparate modelings: the behavior of private, autonomous individuals, and the ubiquitous and inevitable interactions between interdependent individuals.

The critical questions resolved in the ongoing conduct of the economy include: who decides, who can do what to whom, who has what capacity to visit opportunity-set injury or gain on others, and which (whose) impacts?

The situation of interdependence can be modeled as follows. Each economic actor has an opportunity set comprising the array of alternatives open to it. The composition of an individual opportunity set is juxtaposed to the structure of opportunity sets which comprises the distribution of opportunity between individuals or subgroups.

Each opportunity set, both at any point in time and through time, is a result of three sets of forces: power, individual choice, and impacts. By *power* is meant (1) effective participation in decision making and (2) the means or capacity with which to participate in decision making, that is, the bases of participation, such as rights or position, with (2) instrumental to (1). Changes in rights, entitlements, and, inter alia, the rules governing access to and use of rights represent changes in the structure of power and thereby in individual opportunity sets. *Individual choice* connotes the fact that the opportunities open to an individual in the future will reflect, pro tanto, the individual's choices from within past and present opportunity sets. Successful investment will enhance one's holdings of rights-wealth and thereby enlarge one's subsequent opportunity set. The *impacts* of an actor's (or groups of actors' aggregate) choices upon the opportunity sets of other actors may be positive or negative (opportunity enhancing or detracting) and the relationships between the impacting and impacted individual may be zero-sum (one's gain is the other's loss) or positive-sum (the gain to one integrally relating to the gain to the other). The rights underlying power have a dual nature: the protection of alpha's interest is necessarily coupled with an exposure by beta (another individual, subgroup, or the sum of all other individuals) to the exercise of alpha's right. Such exercise by alpha may involve a positive- or zero-sum result but the vesting of the entitlement in alpha is zero-sum from the perspective of beta and beta's nonright. Clearly the process of rights definition and assignment as well as redefinition and reassignment (the process of legal change of law and of private rights) is a major element in interdependence: it is both a source and an instrument of impacts, for example, as some alpha uses government (through voting or lobbying), exercises his or her existing rights to secure new rights thereby visiting a new exposure upon beta. Thus, both the identification and assignment of rights and the exercise of rights creates impacts.

The focus here is on the formation of, interrelations between, and the conditions governing relative opportunity sets. This is in contrast with but includes the conventional analysis of choice from within opportunity sets, which is the second of the three forces discussed above. Morover, the scope of interdependence considered here includes impacts visited through the market (pecuniary externalities and some public goods), outside the market (technological externalities as well as various grants), and through government (sometimes called political externalities and also grants and public goods). The focus is on all impacts and the emphasis is on opportunity sets and impacts consequent to interdependent decision making.

Impacts

General Considerations

Several preliminary but important points should be made. First, impacts are ubiquitous and inevitable because of the fact of interdependence. Second, impacts typically have a reciprocal character in the sense that when alpha and beta are in the same field of action, action by one has impact on the other and preventing impact on the other has impact on the one. (The impact relationship, it will be recalled, may be positive- or zero-sum.) A further contextual meaning of reciprocal relates to the game-theoretic nature of choice: alpha's behavior cannot be determined independent of beta's, inasmuch as alpha's acts depend on (anticipate) beta's, and vice versa.

Third, impacts are selectively perceived and identified. There is selective perception of externalities, public goods, and grants, using the conventional terminology. For example, the pollution externality (impact) may be perceived as such but not the externality (impact) upon the pollutor consequent to pollution control. There also is selective modeling and definition of externality, public good, and grant impacts. Selective perception is a function of (1) the multifaceted character of both theoretical and real-world phenomena, (2) the different perspectives from which both theoretical and real-world phenomena can be approached, (3) the diverse origins of the respective bodies of theory, (4) the diverse uses by analysts, and (5) diverse and often contradictory judgments or presuppositions as to warranted entitlements, goodness and badness, or legitimacy and illegitimacy. Moreover, the identification or recognition of an impact, say, as explicit or implicit; the identification of an impact as positive or negative; and costs and benefits, are all subject to selective perception.

Fourth, selective perception may be a function of position, or power structure, which influences one's life experiences and understandings as well as interests. Fifth, impacts are a partial function of power structure; and impact reversals (often denominated correction or solutions) are a function of power structure (as well as selective perception), and also generate impacts of their own, including the redistribution of power, opportunity, costs, and benefits.

Conditions

The impact of a choice by alpha upon beta clearly is a function of alpha's power and the (defensive) power and ability to choose of beta. There are several other conditions which govern the genesis, and thereby pattern, of impacts. First, technology directly governs the composition and structure of, and interrelationships between opportunity sets, and thereby impacts. Second, the presence and magnitude of exclusion and avoidance costs (transaction costs in general) also directly govern the ability to visit impacts on others and to escape same. Third, the formation of perceptions and preferences directly governs individual choices from within their respective opportunity sets and thereby the impacts produced by such choice. Fourth, individual actors may or may not be able to adjust the quantity of the impact visited upon or available to them. Fifth, physical and sociolegal conditions of appropriability strongly influence the actions and impacts of economic actors. Finally, impacts may be determined by the tenderer or by the receiver; moreover, both the receipt and the tendering may be voluntary or involuntary, and access or exposure may be equal or asymmetrical.

Interdependence arises from technology, the characteristics of goods and of interrelationships among people, and perceptions and preferences. Interdependence resulting from the characteristics of both goods and interrelationships influence how one person's choices can impact on others. If we understand how this interdependence arises, we can understand how alternative rules or rights affect relative opportunity sets and thus the performance of the economy. These characteristics can be grouped and aggregated in various ways depending on the perceived problem.

Interdependence also arises from the character of technology and is subject to change. The same can be said for learned perceptions and preferences. A situation of conflict can be altered in the long run by technological or preference change.

The characteristics of goods—whether they are incompatible use or joint impact—can affect the possibilities for alpha's choices to affect beta's welfare. In all cases, however, the resulting interdependence is affected by technology and preferences. The impact also is affected by group size involved, that is, whether one individual can affect another unilaterally or only in combination with others and whether the number is large or small.

Incompatible use occurs when alpha's use forecloses beta's. This may be seen as technological as in the case of physical incompatibility or as pecuniary as in the case of effect or competition on market price. In some cases alpha can pollute beta (unilateral), or the effect on beta is only felt when many alphas are present (congestion). The situation may differ in the ease with which beta can find a vehicle to create a cost for alpha when alpha visits a cost on beta (degree of reciprocality): for example, alpha is offended on the trip to work by beta's neighborhood deterioration, but beta's trip to work never goes through alpha's neighborhood.

The degree of exclusion cost creates opportunities for beta to ride free on alpha's efforts to create a product. This interdependence obviously is subject to change by technology. It applies to both technological effects (access to products) as well as pecuniary (access to markets). Preferences affect game-theoretic strategy and thus affect impacts.

The interdependence created by high-exclusion cost is affected by group size: the more people, the higher the contractual cost of overcoming free riders. Other sources of transaction costs, such as the cost of information, often are inherent in the good (for example, requiring technical skill in determining quality) and are subject to change by technology.

Joint-impact goods create opportunity for a good created by alpha to be made available to beta without extra cost (the zero marginal cost of additional consumers). It is the polar case of economies of scale, all affected by technology. If the good is desired by all, there is an issue of cost sharing (price or tax differentiation). The problem of reaching agreement (transaction cost) is affected by group size. In the case of economies of scale it is not a matter of unilateral action but aggregation of many choices which affects interdependence. The same is true for variation in supply or demand creating peak loads and rents. Preferences are important since if alpha creates a good, beta can be affected even if she is not asked to cost share when beta has high avoidance costs and cannot adjust quantity independent of alpha's production or use. Even in the case of a grant, when alpha's gift has the potential of improving the giver's and recipient's welfare, it may nevertheless be resented by the recipient.

Classes of Impact Situations: A Tentative Taxonomy

The foregoing distinction between incompatible use and joint-impact goods focuses on characteristics which influence interdependence. Its utility lies in being able to group many different goods which create a particular kind of opportunity for one person's choice to affect others. This means that the kind of institution, rule, or right which controls incompatible use (factor ownership) is different from that which controls joint impact (such as tax incidence or regulated consumption). The outcome or impact of this interdependence can be altered by technology or by changed preferences and is influenced by group size and whether one person can act unilaterally or whether the effect only occurs in some minimum aggregation.

In other problem situations the interaction of alternative rights with characteristics of interdependence to produce a given impact may best be understood by another grouping of the above features. For example, we could focus on whether the effect of one choice or another is a matter of unilateral or aggregative action and whether the interests (preferences) involved are compatible or not. One key in this focus is the role of transaction costs in achieving, avoiding, or sharing the aggregative impact.

A focus on interdependence and impacts suggests a tentative taxonomy of three general types of impact situations, each marked by a particular general type of interrelationship between alphas and betas.

Class I impact situations involve impact arising from the aggregation of simultaneous "independent" actions of alpha and beta. Examples include scale economies, increasing returns within scale, peak loading, congestion, indivisibilities, and game-theoretic strategies. The paradigm case can be seen in terms of increasing returns or congestion: the aggregation of individual actions or choices produces impacts upon each participant which may be positive or negative, a benefit or a cost.

Class II impact situations involve unilateral actions by an individual actor and an incompatibility of use or of interest vis-à-vis another's. Examples include actions producing negative pecuniary, technological, and political externalities and gifts and tribute involuntarily given or received.

Class III impact situations involve unilateral action by an individual actor and compatible use or interest vis-à-vis another's. Examples include actions producing positive externalities, grants voluntarily given or received, and (public) goods wherein provision for one person constitutes provision for another or all others, and consumption by one does not reduce the amount available to others.

The analysis may be elaborated as follows. First, a change in technology may convert a class II to a class III impact, for example, enabling a pollutee to use the pollutant; or a class II to a class I impact, for example, from decreasing to increasing returns. Second, a change in market price may convert a class II to a class III impact, thereby converting a cost to a benefit, for example, enabling the pollutee to sell a pollutant, or eliminating the impact on beta by inducing the hitherto polluting alpha to capture and sell the pollutant.

Third, a change in exclusion or evasion costs may eliminate or otherwise change the pattern of impacts and relationships between parties. Fourth, a change in legal rules may affect appropriability and the costs of exclusion or evasion. Fifth, a change in actor perceptions or preferences may convert a class II to a class III impact, or vice versa.

Sixth, a change in policymaker perceptions or preferences may redefine the control problem from one impact to its reciprocal (from foul air to inability to smoke; from water pollution to inability to produce cheaply or at all; from wildlife or recreational opportunity to housing development; from a tax expenditure to a transfer payment). For example, policymakers may use a narrow or broad definition of injury or of evidence of injury.

Seventh, policies to change economic performance in class I types likely will differ from those attempting to change economic performance in class II and III types. In class I cases, all parties contribute and must either be brought together or separated (always at the margin) to change the impact situation. A pricing system can be used. A pricing system also can be used, among other control alternatives, in class II and III cases. But in class II and III cases the problem of policy is not to separate or bring together the parties but to (re)determine (the means of determining) whose interest is to count insofar as they conflict and who will have the capacity to produce which impacts favorable to themselves and to others. Vis-à-vis class I separability, classes II and III involve reciprocal interdependence as to who can injury or benefit whom. In all three classes, policy decisions may be made with regard to good or bad economic performance independent of the preferences or choices of individual economic actors.

Eighth, interdependent utility functions may be of three types: first, in which alpha's utility enters into beta's utility function; second, in which consumption by alpha means consumption by beta; and third, in which alpha's actions affect beta's learning of preferences, for example, through vicarious or observed experience. Ninth, whereas conventional externality and public-goods theories yield a false sense of determinateness, optimality, and closure, all of which is selective and presumptive, but in each case requiring additional normative premises in order to reach specific externality or public good policies, the present analysis attempts only to identify the types of impact situations which are found in the arenas of interdependence. Whether alpha should be allowed to harm beta, or vice versa; whether the impact defined as "the" problem is downstream pollution or inhibited upstream production; whether one should be unconcerned with the impacts of price-structure change or with impacts which do not lead to further trades, are questions for the economic actors and policymakers, not the neutral analyst.

Conclusion

The present discussion attempts to identify the sources and conditions of interdependence hitherto approached through the theories of externalities, public goods, and grants. It illustrates the ubiquity of interdependence. It suggests that if the ability to affect and be affected by others is many-faceted, then the rights which control them also must be numerous. While factor ownership and degree of competition are important, it is only a partial description of instrumental rights. If we wish to create a certain performance for a chosen interest we will have to group together these types of interdependence so that we can learn from our experience as alternative rights interact with them not only in the short run when technology and preferences can be largely taken as given, but also in the longer-run evolutionary interaction wherein everything is both dependent and interdependent. Depending on the particular group, problem areas, and length of run, the different aspects of interdependence identified by the three bodies of theory can be aggregated or integrated to usefully identify the instrumental role of alternative institutions and rights and to do so without any presumption of whose interests should count.

18 The Political Theory of Public Finance

Larry L. Wade

Traditional textbooks in public finance were careful to circumvent the domain of political theory, content to undertake tasks central to economic analysis and understanding. The first of these was to describe the fiscal system of government; the second was to predict, on the basis of applied price theory, the economic consequences of changes in fiscal rules and allocations; the third was to evaluate various fiscal systems in terms of specified normative or policy objectives: equity, efficiency, employment, and balance of payments. Little theoretical foundation was necessary for the first task, while the second and third rested on Marshallian assumptions concerning the supply of and demand for private goods in the marketplace.

The tremendous expansion in the scope of government beginning in the 1930s, however, seriously undermined the practical advantage of treating government as just another unitary economic actor. Not only had contending forces in liberal polities given rise to an economic decision maker whose behavior could not be explained in traditional terms, government's involvement in a vast range of new undertakings eroded distinctions between the proper functions of the polity and economy maintained in the classical framework.

In this new context, the resulting discomfiture with the limitations of traditional public finance was altogether understandable, and the modern theories of public goods, externalities, and grants, together with the extension of the behavioral assumptions of microeconomic theory to political actors and institutions, have aimed at rectifying what has become a troublesome lacuna in theoretical and practical knowledge. Such efforts have now been incorporated (unsystematically, to be sure) in some public finance texts, and it is one of these statements to which critical attention is directed here. The perspective maintained in this chapter is that of a more-or-less mainstream political scientist with an acquired interest in public finance. As will become clear, greatest criticism is directed at the casual transfer of economic assumptions to political analysis, as well as to the misplaced techniques which have guided economic explanations of political processes bearing on fiscal (and related) questions in liberal governments. One guiding assumption has been that the idealized market could have its analog in the polity, though it has long since been known that this is not at all conceptually warranted.[1] Among the analogous traits which the efficient polity should possess are openness, competition, information, an acceptable distribution of political resources (principally the franchise), and rational, self-interested actors. The task has been thought to consist of the discovery of rules by which individual preferences could be aggregated efficiently as a basis for public policy. One may put aside the fact that many political scientists do not accept the utilitarian ethic which normally animates these efforts, even while indicating other reasons why most of them have such great difficulty accepting, as either descriptions, explanations, or predictions, the fruits of rational-choice, deductive approaches to political decision making. The purpose here is to encourage economists interested in such things to become more alert to the literature of empirical political science and to avoid thereby the temerarious leaps to be found in so much of the economic approach to politics, for it is certainly arguable that a kind of trained incapacity, an inappropriate mind-set, has accompanied the economic forays into political analysis.

One finds such evidence in the justification offered by an eminent scholar, who contends that "the economic model [unlike noneconomic models] is almost entirely predictive in content rather than prescriptive."[2] Hence, given the confusion of noneconomic social scientists vis-à-vis the distinction between prediction and prescription, as well as the "reluctance [of] noneconomic social scientists to undertake rigorous positive examination of behavior patterns, the extension of orthodox economic models to nonmarket behavior seems to fill an awesome gap in social analysis."[3] This is a most peculiar statement, since noneconomic social scientists are as aware as anyone of the difference between prediction and prescription, though they might admit to some confusion over Buchanan's statement that economic models in politics, given their emphasis on efficiency, are without prescriptive content. Buchanan's comment is most startling, however, because the work of most noneconomic social science aims precisely at the rigorous understanding of behavior. Indeed, it is the argument here that economic models in politics have usually neglected, and disastrously so, the rigorous descriptions of political behavior which abound in the political science literature. Contrary to Buchanan's contention, it is often the behavioral assumptions and conclusions of the new public finance which are presented with misguided assurance and empirical ineptitude. One example will suffice before beginning our main task. Elsewhere Buchanan asserts that "clearly, the behavior of the individual as he participates in collective decision processes will depend, and significantly so, on the way his tax bill is presented to him."[4] In point of fact, this is a highly contingent statement, reasonable only under precisely stated conditions; it is not universally true. Obler showed convincingly that a national sample of taxpayers was quite ignorant of the incidence of income, sales, and property taxes, and that both the poor and the rich often favored taxes which self-interest should have led them to oppose.[5] Although Buchanan's rational voter-taxpayer is often sensibly ignorant in the face of fiscal illusions, Obler's taxpayers' ignorance obtained with respect to direct taxes as well. The notion of a rational voter-taxpayer becomes so eroded under these circumstances (and others, as will be shown) as to vitiate any clear reason for its analytical retention. Since all variations in behavior can be explained in the rational model by degrees of uncertainty, the idea that an individual is rational "in the sense that his behavior will be directed toward maximizing his own utility"[6] contains absolutely no predictive power or stable empirical referents; it is, speaking positivisticly, equivalent to saying that "people behave as they behave." It is hard to face the fact that, as simple deductive models are increasingly modified to include more and more important aspects of behavioral and institutional reality, they become indistinguishable from inductive approaches to knowledge. It is not from temperamental or esthetic reasons that most political scientists find rational-choice deductive models unconvincing, but from a conviction that neither prediction nor explanation can be advanced if that reality is not specified in one's analysis. But more than this, the polity cannot resemble the market, first, because of the nature and remoteness of its internal transactions, but also because it is unique socially. It is inherently monopolistic; it is that entity which monopolizes violence or the threat of violence in the community. Power is its organizing principle. As Hamilton wrote in *Federalist 28,* the idea that good republican laws are all that is necessary for its maintenance, is a doctrine to be found "only in the reveries of those political doctors whose sagacity disdains the admonitions of experimental instruction."

There is no dearth of material upon which to draw to illustrate the limitations of the economic/deductive/rational approach in political analysis.[7] For present purposes it is sufficient to select a treatment of politics conveyed in what is properly regarded as a comprehensive and incisive exposition of public finance, the widely adopted text by Richard A. Musgrave and Peggy B. Musgrave, *Public Finance in Theory and Practice,*[8] though the critique developed below is applicable to other writings as well. Indeed, the Musgraves are guilty of rather fewer transgressions against political theory than many others. Recognizing the incontrovertible, that budgeting is a political rather than market process, they seek in their chapter on fiscal politics to consider the political process more closely. The specific questions they pose are precise, empirical, and important: how are the individual's views on fiscal matters expressed and how are they translated into political action; how are fiscal decisions related to political decisions in other areas; what is the role of the party system, of Congress, and of the executive?[9] The political scientist might have anticipated, wrongly in the event, to find subsequent references to the rich and sophisticated literature directed at precisely these questions. But that is not the case. Once stated, the questions are immediately forgotten and attention is directed to the hypothetical problem of "how preferences on the matter can be expressed and implemented."[10] An unacknowledged and mystifying shift occurs from what is to what might be (given rational actors, the canons of logic and alternative decision-rules).

The format takes familiar form. The individual in a binding fiscal referendum will vote his own interest. The old, and still unanswered, question of why a rational individual would vote at all in an electorate of scale is immediately begged in a footnote: "Fortunately, many people do not take this view," acting out of "civic duty" or a desire to "set an example for others."[11] No evidence, incidentally, is cited to support either possibility, introspection being their apparent source. Conceding implicitly at the outset that a utility-maximizing model of voting behavior is flawed, the authors nonetheless persevere to explore what will occur under different distributions of preferences and, for the most part, simple majority rule. When preferences are single-peaked, such a rule makes a winner of that often cited but rarely empirically identified specimen: the median voter. As the Musgraves accurately report, "this simple voting model is the one typically used in designing models of fiscal decision making."[12] Quite so, though the question remains: is this model sufficient, even with amendments, to answer the questions with which the authors began their consideration of the political process? To be sure, the Musgraves make clear that the model will not satisfy all concerns. If preferences are not single-peaked, arbitrary outcomes may result, or inefficiencies may ensue if intensities are not reconciled. But for some fiscal choices (no one knows for which real choices this is true), outcomes may be nonarbitrary, and coalition-formation and logrolling can often accommodate intensities; for some others, unfortunately, single-peakedness will not obtain and collective paradoxes will emerge. These latter problems can be minimized by the artful combining of issues by politicians; in fact, "it is the function of the politician to identify and present such bundles or political programs."[13]

Observe what has happened. From a simple analytical model, undisturbed by reference to empirical research and resting precariously on dubious behavioral assumptions, the reader is led to the empirical observation that it is the function of the politician to resolve problems posed in what is merely a theoretical construct. Since it cannot be contended seriously that the actual function (in the sociological sense) of politicians is to solve entirely formal problems, charity requires the conclusion that something else is meant. What must be intended is that it would somehow be a nicer, more preferable world if politicians were to seek to render majority rule less arbitrary than formal reasoning suggests it might sometimes be. What is under discussion is not the political process of political science which the Musgraves wish to examine more closely, but one which is data-free, fictional, stylized, prescriptive (and, as will be shown, lacking in internal consistency). Voting, it is recognized from the model, typically entails losers and consequent loss of welfare. To minimize this problem, a search is encouraged for voting solutions that are least defective, that is, will most closely approximate the actual preferences of voters. If the Musgraves had then turned to an examination of actual real-world preferences, however, their search for efficient rules would have been irrevocably crushed against the most perplexing facts. A vast body of evidence reveals that individual preferences on public questions are often unknown, nonexistent, unstable, contradictory, unrealistic, variously distributed, or pitched at such a high level of abstraction as to be unhelpful to decision makers (for example, the government should reduce unemployment or free the hostages). Not only is popular knowledge of concrete policy problems extremely limited,[14] but, regrettably, public opinion can be exceedingly dangerous and illiberal and best combated or ignored by policymakers on prudential grounds.[15] Among other reasons, market analogies have limited applicability in politics because voting provides individuals the opportunity to choose for the community as well as themselves. Individual preferences and self-interest can reasonably be given free reign in the marketplace, and the resulting efficiencies can be appropriately applauded, since bad judgment will affect only the participants. In the polity the situation is vastly different, and checks against popular majorities are not always unreasonable. Many political scientists would share Madison's view (and virtually all others would give it careful attention) in *Federalist 51,* that "In forming a government . . . the great difficulty lies in this: You must first enable the government to control the governed; and in the next place oblige it to control itself." Obviously, the Musgraves and Madison are concerned to find rules to achieve very different objectives. The control of power, not efficiency, was the first concern of Madison. The discrepancy between economic and political reasoning could scarcely be posed more sharply than in this instance.

Having informed their reader of the several analytic problems associated with voting as a means of aggregating preferences efficiently, the Musgraves seek to make their discussion of the political process more realistic by examining the theory of representative democracy. Again little or no empirical information is conveyed in addressing the question: if representatives are now added to the model, how will the preferences of individuals be reflected in final decisions? Joseph Schumpeter (who sketched) and Anthony Downs (who developed in detail) are cited as important figures who extended the notion of "homo economicus" (that is, rational utility-maximizing voters and politicians) to an interpretation of the political process. Politicians seek to maximize votes in order to get or retain office; citizens vote for the politician or party offering the most attractive tax-expenditure package. In point of fact, Schumpeter held no such presumptions, his effort being to contribute to an empirical theory of democracy, not a formal or analytic one. He wrote, for example, that "our chief troubles about the classical theory centered in the proposition that 'the people' have a definite and rational opinion about every individual question and that they give effect to this opinion . . . in a democracy . . . by choosing 'representatives' who will see to it that that opinion is carried out.''[16]

Schumpeter's concern was to establish a practical test by which one could identify an empirically defined democracy. If politicians compete for votes through regular elections, a political system will so qualify. The relationship between voter preferences and policy decisions was an entirely different matter: as the citizen "enters the political field . . . he argues and analyzes in a way which he would readily recognize as infantile within the sphere of his real interests . . . He becomes a primitive again."[17] Obviously Schumpeter is not discussing homo economicus. In fact, two more dissimilar views of voter competence can scarcely be found than those presented by Schumpeter and Downs. The Downsian theory takes one away from Schumpeter's empiricism into the world of formal models. The theory is familiar enough and need not be restated here except to note that uncertainty is introduced at whatever points are necessary to explain apparent deviations from rational political behavior.[18] Uncertainty can accommodate all the facts which an empirical science seeks to identify, measure, and weight in a system of causal reasoning. As the concept expands, the model's facade dissolves into a sea of induction and no sensible test remains by which to distinguish rational from irrational behavior.

Political change is similarly understood on deductive (and often erroneous) grounds, with the Musgraves' behavioral assertions advanced entirely without reference to the relevant literature. If the governing party (team) loses, it is said to be because of the voting paradox, poor implementation of the platform upon which it was elected (as if platforms were always intended to be implemented or voters were aware of such statements), poor estimates as to citizen preferences, changing voter preferences, and poor leadership. "For these and other reasons . . . continuous change may result."[19] Much as a black hole, these statements on political change absorb everything. But is it conceivable change in the model or the existential change in the real world that is identified? Only in the model, for the actual sources of political change are still poorly understood and cannot be adduced on the basis of a logic required of a hypothetical model. For real insights into changes in party dominance, the reader is more properly directed to the empirical studies of political transformation and the innumerable testable propositions they contain.[20] It is the task of science to state conditions, not enumerate possibilities.

Having dealt with political change, several logical exercises are presented which have implications for the Musgraves' theory of democracy. A three-voter model, involving two issues, each carrying two options which can be ranked cardinally, is introduced to show that majority rule can accommodate intensities. Since the model is psychologically unsound (voters do not, as far as is known, assign hypothetical points to various preferences) and inconsistent with the way issues are normally perceived in the real world, it resides entirely in the prescriptive/analytic realm. The problem is that, in context, it is presented as if democratic politics operated on its principles. The Musgraves are careful to point out that this model, though it ranks intensities, does not involve an interpersonal comparison of utility. But when logrolling is discussed, such comparisons are introduced without acknowledgment. In a three-person logrolling model, two voters are allowed to trade votes so that each receives his most preferred outcome. The third person "loses as a result, but for the values shown [in the example] the gain obtained by X and Z exceeds Y's loss . . . intensity of feeling comes to be allowed for and results in a more efficient choice."[21] The interpersonal welfare comparison is required to show that, by linking issues, logrolling can be an efficient procedure. No effort is made to demonstrate that logrolling in actual politics fulfills their efficiency requirement nor, strictly speaking, could they do so, given the utilitarian individualism upon which the concept of efficiency rests and the Musgraves' inexplicable resort to interpersonal comparisons.

In any case, far from being disreputable the linking of issues, according to the Musgraves, "is thus an essential and useful part of the political process," and may involve not only "fiscal issues such as highway construction or tax rates" but "other issues, such as school prayer or busing."[22] The reference to such contemporary issues suggests that the Musgraves are saying something about the real world, but in the absence of institutional facts the illustration is empirically pointless and normatively unsound. Mandatory school busing and school prayer have been treated as constitutional issues over which parliamentarians are not free to bargain, and the judicial process, through which such issues are addressed, is not susceptible to issue-linkages of the sort contemplated. One has the greatest doubt that the Musgraves would contend upon mature reflection that civil rights and liberties should be linked to highway construction tax rates in the interest of efficiency, but it is to such conclusions that uncritical modeling leads them.

In considering another aspect of republicanism, the Musgraves assert that the large-number case (the electorate) applies to the small-number case (the legislature), since the "bargaining of each representative [is] constrained, more-or-less narrowly, by the preferences of his large number of constituents."[23] Since it has been shown that this is very far from the truth in American politics,[24] the assertion has neither empirical nor predictive value and must be presumed to have prescriptive intent. The fact is, that if the actual voting latitude enjoyed by legislators were admitted, the formal model, which leads to such desirable outcomes, would either have to be discarded altogether or so modified as to reveal the actual inefficiency of the political process. It is understandable that advocates of democracy, as defined by the Musgraves, might be reluctant to make the required concession, for to do so is to reject the methodology, the model, and a particular understanding of democracy to which some scholars are wedded.

To be sure, the Musgraves do allude to some real-world problems with the delegate model. Voting rights are still in question as concerns voting age (the twenty-sixth amendment, 1971, perhaps did not go far enough) and literacy requirements, as well as the availability of registration and voting facilities.[25] Such restraints on entry are held to inhibit the optimal working of the polity in the same way that industrial organization, and so on, can distort market outcomes. Such extraordinary comparisons illustrate the perversity of reasoning from analogy. To regard registration, literacy, and age rules as necessarily subversive of optimal democracy is to advance an arbitrary, even peculiar, view—government by public opinion—altogether inconsistent with those democratic thinkers who have regarded an informed electorate as indispensable to a successful democracy.

The ideal polity is further undermined, according to the Musgraves, moving onto exceedingly slippery ground, by the existence of political parties which restrict competition much like, one gathers, oligopoly in the economy. Distortions are introduced because representatives are subject to party discipline, though it is "relatively mild in the United States."[26] It is asserted that, with party discipline, "representatives may be unable to reflect the preferences of their constituents," and "in the absence of proportional representation . . . an absolute majority must be obtained within the electoral district, a difficult task for new or minority groups."[27] This is not only factually wrong (a plurality is sufficient to win congressional and most other legislative elections in the United States), but neglects to observe that, in a two-party competition, the electorate chooses the government. In a multiparty parliamentary system, governments may be formed by party leaders after the election, and it is not clear why coalition-formation within the parties before the election is inferior on efficiency grounds to coalition-formation after the election. Indeed, the first situation would seem to present the voters both with more influence and information than the latter one. Far from restricting competition, parties organize it, make it visible and institutional, provide information, and increase turnout.[28]

As it happens, American parties are in a state of considerable decay, a state consistent with the Musgraves' preferences if one exceedingly worrisome to many others who see some virtue in disciplined political parties. The Downsian scheme, which the Musgraves regard as more or less accurate, does of course require discipline even while the brute facts are otherwise. For example, if a strict test of team voting in the House of Representatives is a situation in which at least 90 percent of the Republicans vote in opposition to 90 percent of the Democrats, then only some 3 percent of all votes taken in recent years qualify (down from over 50 percent in the late-nineteenth century). A loose test, in which 50 percent of each party is opposed to the other, is now met only about 40 percent of the time (down from nearly 80 percent in 1897–1899).[29]

Nor are deviations from party voting punished by constituencies: from 1952 to 1974 only 5 percent of incumbent senators and less than 2 percent of incumbent representatives were defeated in party primaries. Nor were incumbent rascals thrown out for the failures of their parties; only 6 percent of incumbent House members were defeated in general elections in the same twenty-two-year period.[30] For the representative voter, parties are not at all regarded as teams offering contrasting combinations of public policies. The Downsian voter is required to cast his ballot for the party that "he believes will provide him with a higher utility income than any other party during the coming election period."[31] Obviously, the tremendous rise in split-ticket voting, combined with chronic majorities in Congress and shifting party control of the White House considerably qualifies the team concept essential to the Downsian formulation.

A recent study, using more disaggregated data than conventionally employed, showed no linear relationship between changes in the vote for individual congressional candidates and changes in real income and inflation at the district level in the 1972, 1974, and 1976 elections, even though, according to survey data, economic conditions were the greatest concern of the public during those years.[32] Economic conditions do appear to affect presidential elections, though under what conditions and to what extent remain unclear.[33] However, even if it is the president who is held accountable for economic conditions and tax-expenditure impacts, the utility-maximizing voter would partly be wrong in doing so, since tax policy is a jealously guarded congressional prerogative,[34] and monetary authorities do not always accede to presidential direction. Given behavioral and institutional facts such as these, the predictive/explanatory value of simplistic economic models in politics approaches zero.

If the political process is to be explained with economic analytics, models will have to be far more subtle, complex, and informed than at present. Time and again voting studies have shown that voting decisions are a function of short-term tendencies (personalities of candidates, economic and cultural issues) and long-term forces (partisanship, social class, a variety of demographic variables). Only when these factors are modeled along with appropriate institutional variables will the world of real politics be more amenable to explanation and prediction.

The discrepancy between the induction of political science and the deduction of economics is apparent too in the Musgraves' discussion of the size of the public sector. Their own view is that it is about right relative to popular preferences, but two other schools of thought are cited: the first holds to an underexpansion hypothesis (government is too small), the second to an overexpansion one (government is too large); all three views, as presented, are based upon presumptions and speculation, not empirical research. As concerns the possibility of underexpansion, Pigou is cited to the effect that, "A voting system, with compulsory application of the winning policy, is needed if social goods are to be provided for at all."[35] This view rests upon a number of prior assumptions (involving voluntarism, markets, and so on) which are insensitive to history. All governments, with or without voting institutions, provide some social goods in some degree, and some autocratic or totalitarian ones have done so lavishly. Pigou's point, which is essentially normative, is advanced as an empirical proposition. It is well-known that no efficient rules governing the optimal supply of social goods exist, for reasons which are both technical and practical. Whatever the size of government, its evaluation is most properly based upon a normative system other than that used conventionally to evaluate market efficiency.

If voter-taxpayers are biased against public goods because their benefits are less visible than their costs, the polity is said to be too small. Conversely, if taxes are hidden, if expenditure decisions are not linked to tax decisions, or if concentrated benefits can be secured while costs are distributed, the polity is regarded as too large. The problem with such explanations is not only that they are merely conjectural and oblivious to the actual processes which establish public sector activity. Both hypotheses are based on a simple model of policy outcomes in which voter-taxpayers are differentially ignorant. If properly informed, they would establish different demands (and politicians would presumably honor them); that is, if people and institutions were different than what they are, they would behave differently. The political scientist is apt to find very little of this useful or interesting. If the question is whether citizens view government as too large, too small, or about right, the appropriate strategy of discovery is survey research. If the question is how expansionary public programs are instituted or blocked, detailed case studies are in order. In such efforts, the impact of events, social structure, culture, power, issues, and institutions may yield decisive answers, while weak metaphors are not always helpful.

This is not to say that there are no links between public opinion and public policy. There assuredly are, but they are not of the sort depicted in the economic models. On some few highly salient issues, a more-or-less direct linkage may obtain,[36] but this is not conventional. For the most part, as noted, voters are characterized by "widespread ignorance and indifference over matters of policy,''[37] and are frequently misled by politicians as to the real nature of current issues.[38] Candidates for office engage in rhetoric, "often designed [as much] to subvert as to facilitate rational voting behavior. What candidates say frequently lacks relevance to any decision [which] voters face, expose differences in the views of candidates imperfectly, and is fitted with evasions, ambiguities and distortions."[39] Such awareness led one political scientist to argue that it is typically irrational for a politician to disseminate correct information to voters; if there are informed voters, there must be irrational politicians.[40] For the vast majority of issues, the connections between citizen preferences and policy are weak or nonexistent.[41]

In the complex real world, mass opinion can sometimes be a source of policy, but it may also be a reflection of policy, a constraint on policy, or irrelevant to policy.[42] Citizen preferences may dominate on those occasions when politicians perceive correctly what a majority wants, when issues are salient to a majority, and when politicians are given incentives to act consistently with majority preferences. Issues involving mass unemployment, social security, or an acute international crisis may be cases in point.[43] Alternatively, major policy initiatives can be taken in the absence of popular majorities, as occurs regularly with foreign policy decisions, or as occurred with automobile safety or environmental protection, where legislation was passed before popular demand had formed.[44] There are innumerable instances in which officials are at liberty to act without reference to public opinion "provided they do not publicly violate procedural norms—fairness, honesty, and due regard for the apparent interests of the many."[45] Or majority opinion is often ignored altogether, as with mandatory school busing to achieve racial integration, minority hiring quotas, capital punishment, or the Electoral College.[46]

The Musgraves do allude to several alternative explanations of public finance decisions, including Marxist views, an (ill-informed) interest-group approach, several utopian philosophies, and a few recent empirical studies. Attention here has been restricted to the very serious limitations of any rational-choice deductive approach which ignores or mistakes what is known to be true of political processes. Those who wish to follow a rational choice approach will find their models improved and their results more acceptable only if some alertness is shown to the polity as it is. The political science literature is not inaccessible and a beginning is suggested in the notes to this chapter. As it is, the median-voter metaphor and attendant assumptions about political behavior verge on mythology. "Myths cast the real world in such general terms that they reduce complex relations to simple propositions anchored as much in faith as in serious reality testing." Myths make it "easy to find confirming evidence . . . and difficult to see the relevance of other information at all."[47]

Notes

1. See Richard Zeckhauser, "Voting Systems, Honest Preferences and Pareto Optimality," *American Political Science Review* 67 (September 1973): 934–946.

2. James M. Buchanan, "Toward Analysis of Closed Behavioral Systems," in *Theory of Public Choice,* ed. James M. Buchanan and Robert P. Tollison, (Ann Arbor: University of Michigan Press, 1972), p. 17.

3. Ibid., p. 18.

4. James M. Buchanan, *Public Finance in Democratic Process* (Chapel Hill: University of North Carolina Press, 1967), p. 17.

5. Jeffrey Obler, "The Odd Compartmentalization: Public Opinion, Aggregate Data and Policy Analysis," *Policy Studies Journal* 7 (Spring 1979): 524–537.

6. Buchanan, *Public Finance in Democratic Process,* p. 9.

7. See L.L. Wade, "Public Administration, Public Choice, and the Pathos of Reform," *Review of Politics* 41 (July 1979): 344–374.

8. 2d ed. (New York: McGraw-Hill, 1976).

9. Ibid., chapter 5.

10. Ibid., p. 103.

11. Ibid.

12. Ibid., p. 105.

13. Ibid., p. 109.

14. Among many studies, see W. Lance Bennett, *Public Opinion in American Politics* (New York: Harcourt Brace Jovanovich, 1980).

15. Two classic studies on this theme are Samuel A. Stauffer, *Communism, Conformity, and Civil Liberties* (Garden City, N.Y.: Doubleday, 1954), and James W. Prothro and Charles M. Grigg, "Fundamental Principles of Democracy: Bases of Agreement and Disagreement," *Journal of Politics* 22 (Spring 1960): 275–292.

16. Joseph A. Schumpeter, *Capitalism, Socialism and Democracy* (New York: Harper Torchbooks, 1962), p. 269.

17. Ibid., p. 262.

18. Anthony Downs, *An Economic Theory of Democracy* (New York: Harper & Row, 1957).

19. Musgrave and Musgrave, *Public Finance,* p. 112.

20. Particularly useful studies of changing party dominance include James L. Sundquist, *Dynamics of the Party System* (Washington, D.C.: Brookings Institution, 1973), and Walter Dean Burnham, *Critical Elections and the Mainsprings of American Politics* (New York: Norton, 1970).

21. Musgrave and Musgrave, *Public Finance,* p. 114.

22. Ibid., p. 115.

23. Ibid.

24. Empirical studies of constituency/legislator connections include Warren E. Miller and Donald E. Stokes, "Constituency Influences in Congress," *American Political Science Review* 57 (March 1963): 45–56; Lewis A. Dexter, "The Representative and His District," in T. Lowi and R. Ripley, eds., *Legislative Politics U.S.A.* (Boston: Little, Brown, 1973), pp. 175–184; and Charles F. Cnudde and Donald J. McCrone, "The Linkage between Constituency Attitudes and Congressional Voting Behavior: A Causal Model," *American Political Science Review* p. 60 (March 1966): 66–72.

25. Musgrave and Musgrave, *Public Finance,* p. 115.

26. Ibid., p. 116.

27. Ibid.

28. See Frank Sorauf, *Party Politics in America,* 3d ed. (Boston: Little, Brown, 1976), p. 8.

29. Joseph Cooper, David Brady, and Patricia Hurley, "The Electoral Basis of Party Voting," in *The Impact of the Electoral Process,* ed. Louis Maisel and Joseph Cooper, (Beverly Hills, Calif.: Sage, 1977), p. 139.

30. Walter Dean Burnham, "American Politics in the 70's," in *The American Party Systems,* ed. W.N. Chambers and W.D. Burnham, 2d ed. (New York: Oxford, 1975), p. 321.

31. Downs, *Economic Theory of Democracy,* pp. 38–39.

32. John R. Owens and Edward C. Olson, "Economic Fluctuations and Congressional Elections," *American Journal of Political Science* 24 (August 1980).

33. Morris P. Fiorina, "Economic Retrospective Voting in American National Elections: A Microanalysis," *American Journal of Political Science* 22 (May 1978): 426–443.

34. George Goodwin, *The Little Legislatures* (Amherst: University of Massachusetts Press, 1970).

35. Musgrave and Musgrave, *Public Finance,* p. 117.

36. W. Lance Bennett, *Public Opinion in American Politics* (New York: Harcourt Brace Jovanovich, 1980), pp. 122–123.

37. Angus Campbell et al., *The American Voter* (New York: Wiley, 1960), p. 186.

38. Benjamin I. Page and Richard A. Brody, "Policy Voting and the Electoral Process: The Vietnam War Issue," *American Political Science Review* 66 (September 1972): 995.

39. Stanley Kelley, Jr., *Political Campaigning* (Washington, D.C.: Brookings Institution, 1960), p. 51.

40. Benjamin I. Page, "The Theory of Political Ambiguity," *American Political Science Review* 70 (September 1976): 742–752.

41. Bennett, *Public Opinion in American Politics,* p. 123.

42. James Q. Wilson, *American Government* (Lexington, Mass.: D.C. Heath and Co., 1980), p. 128.

43. Robert S. Erikson and Norman R. Luttbeg, *American Public Opinion* (New York: Wiley, 1973), pp. 41–42.

44. Wilson, *American Government,* p. 129.

45. Ibid.

46. Ibid.

47. Bennett, *Public Opinion in American Politics,* p. 27.

Index

About the Contributors

Barry Ames is an associate professor in the Department of Political Science at Washington University, St. Louis. He previously taught at the University of New Mexico and received the Ph.D. degree from Stanford University. His recent publications include "The Politics of Public Spending in Latin America" and *Rhetoric and Reality in a Militarized Regime: Brazil after 1964.*

Gerald E. Auten is associate professor of economics at Bowling Green State University. During 1978–1979 he was a Brookings Economic Policy Fellow in the Office of Tax Analysis, U.S. Treasury Department, where most of the research include capital-gains taxes and state tax-revenue-forecasting models. Professor Auten's work has appeared in various professional journals, including *National Tax Journal, International Economic Review,* and *Public Finance Quarterly.*

Patrick Cooper is a graduate student in the Center for Public Policy Studies at the University of Wisconsin–Madison and has worked on taxes and budgetary issues for the Wisconsin Department of Natural Resources.

Peter Formuzis is associate professor of economics at California State University, Fullerton. His recent publications include "Bank Capital: The Deposit-Protection Incentive" (with Benjamin M. Friedman) in *Journal of Bank Research* and "The Demand for Euro-dollars and the Optimum Stock of Bank Liabilities" in *Journal of Money, Credit, and Banking.*

William F. Fox is assistant professor of finance at the University of Tennessee. His published work is related to the financing and provision of government services and rural economic development.

Michael L. Goetz is assistant professor of economics at Temple University. His recent publications include articles in *Southern Economic Journal* and *Land Economics.* His current research interests include the development of models of zoning, an economic analysis of the "takings" issue, and the causes and dimensions of changes in regional industrial activity.

Susan B. Hansen is a lecturer in political science at the University of Michigan and a research investigator in the Center for Political Studies. Ms. Hansen has published articles on participation, women's politics, and tax policy. She is now completing a book entitled *The Politics of Taxation.*

187

Mark W. Huddleston is assistant professor of political science at the University of Delaware. He writes in the area of public administration and budgeting, and is currently conducting more extensive research on the policy impacts of the 1974 Congressional Reform and Impoundment Control Act.

Edward T. Jennings, Jr., is an assistant professor and director of the Master's Program in Public Policy and Administration in the Political Science Department at the State University of New York at Buffalo. Professor Jennings's recent publications include "Competition, Constituencies, and Welfare Policies in American States" in *American Political Science Review* and "Urban Riots and Welfare Policy: A Test of the Piven-Cloward Theory" in *Why Policies Succeed or Fail.*

Henry C. Kenski is an associate professor in the Department of Political Science at the University of Arizona. His recent publications include "Partisanship, Ideology, and Constituency Differences on Environmental Issues in the U.S. House of Representatives: 1973–78" (with Margaret Corgan Kenski) in *Policy Studies Journal,* "Economic Perception and Presidential Popularity: A Comment" in *Journal of Politics,* and "The Impact of Unemployment on Congressional Elections, 1958–74: A Cross-Sectional Analysis" in *American Politics Quarterly.*

David Lowery is assistant professor of political science in the Martin School of Public Administration at the University of Kentucky. His research interests include the politics of taxation, public budgeting, and evaluation research.

Margaret McKay is assistant professor of political science at Seton Hall University. She received the Ph.D. from the University of California, Riverside, in 1978. Her fields of interest include public policy, urban politics, and public administration.

Attiat F. Ott is professor of economics at Clark University and Adjunct Scholar of the American Enterprise Institute. Among her many contributions to the economics literature are *Federal Budget Policy* and *Macroeconomic Theory* (with D. Ott and J. Yoo).

Kent E. Portney, assistant professor of political science at Tufts University, received the Ph.D. in government from Florida State University in 1979. He has published articles in education finance and in judicial politics. Dr. Portney's current research interests include political aspects of state tax decisions, intergovernmental fiscal relations, and issues of political economy.

Anil Puri is assistant professor of economics at California State University, Fullerton. He is the author of "Indexing Income Tax for Inflation: The California Experiment" in *Los Angeles Business and Economics,* forthcoming.

Robert H. Rasche is professor of economics at Michigan State University. Professor Rasche's recent work has appeared in various journals, including *Journal of Monetary Economics, Econometrica,* and *Journal of Money, Credit, and Banking.*

J. Norman Reid received the Ph.D. degree from the University of Illinois-Urbana in 1975 and is currently with the Economic Development Division, U.S. Department of Agriculture. He is interested in a broad range of issues relating to federal, state, and local government organization and policies. Dr. Reid's research has included the study of the causes and effects of federal spending. He is presently completing a study of substate regionalism.

A. Allan Schmid is professor of agricultural economics and resource development at Michigan State University. He teaches courses in public-affairs management, public choice, and benefit-cost analysis. He is the author of *Property, Power, and Public Choice.*

Ronald L. Teigen received the B.B.A. and the M.A. degrees from the University of Minnesota and received the Ph.D. degree from the Massachusetts Institute of Technology. Dr. Teigen is currently professor of economics at the University of Michigan. He has been a visiting professor at a number of European universities and was Deputy Assistant Director for Fiscal Analysis, Congressional Budget Office during 1975–1976. His recent publications include "Flow and Stock Equilibrium in a Dynamic Metzler Model" (with William H. Branson in *Journal of Finance,* "Demand and Supply Functions for Money: Another Look at Theory and Measurement" in *Econometrica,* and "Federal Financial Reporting," Congressional Budget Office Technical Paper.

Henry C. Wallich is a member of the Board of Governors, Federal Reserve System, and a frequent contributor to professional journals and books on monetary issues.

About the Editors

Warren J. Samuels is professor of economics at Michigan State University, where he teaches courses in public-expenditure theory, the history of economic thought, and comparative economic systems. He is editor of *Journal of Economic Issues* and in 1980–1981 is president-elect of the History of Economics Society. In addition to numerous articles and book reviews in professional journals, he has published *The Classical Theory of Economic Policy* and *Pareto on Policy*. He coauthored *Law and Economics: An Institutionalist Perspective* (with A. Allan Schmid), forthcoming.

Larry L. Wade is professor of political science at the University of California, Davis, where he teaches courses in American politics, policy analysis, and systematic political theory. His publications include articles in scholarly journals and a number of books, among them *The Elements of Public Policy, Economic Development of South Korea, A Logic of Public Policy,* and *A Theory of Political Exchange.*